WAR in the Garden of Eden

A Military Chaplain's Memoir from Baghdad

Frank E. Wismer III

SEABURY BOOKS
New York

Interior design by Scribe Inc.
Cover design by Laurie Klein Westhafer
Cover photos by the author

Library of Congress Cataloging-in-Publication Data

Wismer, Frank E.
War in the Garden of Eden : a military chaplain's memoir from Baghdad / Frank E. Wismer III.
p. cm.
ISBN 978-1-59627-103-6 (pbk.)
1. Iraq War, 2003—Personal narratives, American. 2. United States—Politics and government—2001– 3. Wismer, Frank E. 4. Military chaplains—United States—Biography. I. Title.
DS79.76.W568 2008
956.7044'37—dc22
[B] 2008021235

Seabury Books
445 Fifth Avenue
New York, New York 10016
www.seaburybooks.com

An imprint of Church Publishing Incorporated

5 4 3 2 1

Contents

Dedication

My return to the United States from Operation Desert Storm in 1991 entailed an incredible experience. Shortly before our plane landed in Bangor, Maine, our flight attendant suggested that we might want to enter the terminal in formation as a unit. We formed up four or five abreast and marched down (literally) into the concourse. When the front rank of our formation became visible to the people in the concourse, a cheer went up, and the high school band started playing. Hundreds of people were present to greet us, offer us food and drink, and invite us to use a telephone to call home. Dozens of people had T-shirts that they wanted us to autograph. We were treated like celebrities. It was astounding. It was also 0600 hours on a Friday morning. These folks had been up for hours preparing to greet our flight.

The people of Maine have greeted every returning flight flying into Bangor from a combat theater with U.S. military personnel aboard since 1991. They also greet the flights of military personnel deploying to the theater of operations. I have flown through Bangor four times during my deployments to Southwest Asia. The lovely people of Bangor have welcomed me each time. They have given flesh to the notion that America supports its men and women in the armed services and made that phrase much more than a cliché. It is to them that I dedicate this book.

Preface

I kept a daily journal during my year in Baghdad, Iraq. I wanted to be certain that I would have the opportunity to "process" my experiences following my deployment as an Army chaplain. The daily life of today's military personnel in a combat theater of operations is not composed of days and weeks of boredom punctuated by moments of stark terror. The life of U.S. military personnel is a demanding, grueling, and relentless fourteen- to eighteen-hour-a-day job that does not recognize weekends and holidays. Military personnel who are deployed to a combat theater of operations quickly discover that there is little time for personal pursuits or interests. Yet deployment to a combat theater is a life-altering experience that significantly impacts the psyche and behavior of those who survive it.

The purpose of this book is twofold. First, I wrote it to permit myself to integrate the experiences of war into the rest of my life. Military personnel deployed to a combat zone quickly discover that they live two lives. There is life in the "sandbox," and there is life back in the world. Rarely do these two lives intersect. I recently spoke to a veteran of the first Gulf War who informed me that he still has not worked through his thoughts and feelings. He participated in the slaughter of Iraqi military personnel on the "highway of death" as they attempted to flee Kuwait. He explained to me that he was much too busy at work to think about that now.

The chapters of this book are not a chronological account of my deployment to Baghdad from April of 2003 to May of 2004. The accounts of this book might be considered a tapestry, for in it I have attempted to weave the threads of 2003–2004 into the larger picture of my life experience. Soldiers are fond of saying, "What happens in Iraq stays in Iraq [or wherever else they are deployed]!" What I have discovered about myself is that I've got to take me with me wherever I go. Keeping a journal in Baghdad and then putting my experiences to paper in the form of a book has been a cathartic experience for me.

The second reason for writing this book is to invite the reader into my "foxhole." I would like to share with the reader a sense of what it is like to be mobilized and deployed to a combat theater of operations. I would like to share with the reader a sense of military life as I experienced it and the role of a chaplain within the military. I would like to give others a sense of daily life in Baghdad when it was the "center of gravity" in world history. I would like the reader to taste the desert air and the flavor of Iraq. I would like the reader to meet some of the extraordinary individuals who shaped my life and sustained me during my year in Baghdad and who shared the challenges and hardships I faced.

—Chaplain (Colonel, retired) Frank E. Wismer III, USAR

Acknowledgment

I am continually thankful for the people of St. George's Anglican Church and the Reverend Canon Andrew White who nurtured and supported me during my twelve and a half months in Iraq. Their fidelity to God, their struggle to achieve peace, and their joy-filled countenances in the midst of the horrors of life in Baghdad continue to be an inspiration to me. This book is written in grateful thanksgiving for all that they have given to me.

Chapter 1

Katja Bullock

The U.S. military plans and conducts its missions on three distinct levels. First, there is the tactical level. Simply put, tactics are the purview of those elements within the military that will engage and destroy the enemy and also of those units directly supporting the "war fighter." We call these elements maneuver units. These are the units that maneuver on the battlefield. Basic training in the Army is designed to train new recruits to function at the tactical level. Following basic training, soldiers will spend a significant portion of their military careers rehearsing the skills required to succeed on the battlefield.

The greatest tactical advantage enjoyed by the U.S. military, in my opinion, is not that we have frightening firepower or that we possess "smart" bombs. It isn't that we have the most advanced weapons systems or even that we have the best training. The scariest thing about the U.S. military in my generation and our greatest tactical advantage is that we can see on the battlefield at night. Our technology allows us to fight at night as if it is day. In other words, we can conduct our tactics twenty-four hours a day without interruption. Our enemies can no longer hide from us on the battlefield at night. This is what makes the U.S. military truly frightening. The U.S. military has become a relentless adversary twenty-four hours a day.

The intermediate plane on which the U.S. military conducts its missions is the operational level. Operational planning ensures that all the tactical components interact successfully in order to accomplish the mission objectives. What immediately comes to my mind when I think of operations is getting the men and material together at the right time and place along with a well-conceived plan for mission accomplishment. The U.S. military today has the operational sophistication to leverage all its assets in a coordinated effort to achieve success. No longer are the Army, Navy, Marine Corps, Air Force, and Coast Guard independent organizations each with their own direction and agenda. Our branches of service are highly integrated partners in a coordinated effort to accomplish the task at hand. Today's military is also prepared to conduct missions at every point along the operational continuum. Operational planning ranges from peacekeeping operations to low-intensity conflict to full-scale war to "nation building."

Finally, the U.S. military conducts warfare at the strategic level. Strategic planning is the "big picture" approach to the deployment and employment of U.S. forces in the theater of operations. One example of U.S. military strategic planning is highlighted by the change in our approach to the utilization of military units. During the Cold War, the U.S. military was "forward deployed." That is to say that we had hundreds of thousands of troops stationed in western Europe. The units to which these troops belonged were headquartered in Europe and remained there while the troops themselves rotated in and out of those units. Today's military is a "power projection" force. That is to say, U.S. military personnel are stationed, for the most part, in the United States and then forward deployed as mission dictates. In the next few years, most of our units stationed in Germany will be headquartered in CONUS (the continental United States). Our military is in the process of becoming a more agile, highly mobile force that is capable of responding quickly to any world crisis. Within hours, we can deploy troops with the skills and equipment necessary to provide humanitarian relief or conduct combat operations.

✣

The Global War on Terrorism (GWOT) requires a global strategy if the United States is to be successful. It requires leaders who are capable of thinking, planning, and acting at strategic rather than tactical levels. I am becoming more and more convinced that the United States is engaged in a "global war" with a discernable strategic plan aimed at mission accomplishment. When I read between the lines regarding the invasion of Iraq, our strategic plan comes into focus. I find it noteworthy that our national debate regarding the GWOT does not engage our strategic objectives. The fact of the matter is that our national debate never seems to look at the "big picture." I sometimes wonder, therefore, if I'm delusional and just imagining that we have a strategic plan. Am I one of the bystanders telling the emperor that he's got a lovely new suit of clothes while he's roaming around in his underwear?

The level of our national debate seems to revolve around the number of U.S. casualties in Iraq (not an insignificant issue) and how we can get out of there in the quickest manner possible. In other words, our national debate is a discussion at the tactical level of warfare. It attempts to compel us to make strategic decisions for tactical reasons. This is certainly not a blueprint for the success of a nation involved in a global war.

✣

Katja Bullock

The Coalition Provisional Authority (CPA), and its antecedent, the Organization for Reconstruction and Humanitarian Assistance (ORHA), was a complex interagency and intergovernmental organism. It was composed of White House staffers, Pentagon planners, and State Department officials. It included Iraqi Americans who possessed the expertise to reestablish the institutions of the government in Iraq and it contained foreign military and civilian personnel representing partner nations in the U.S.-led coalition.

The Coalition Provisional Authority was reliant upon a highly skilled team of U.S. and foreign military and civilian personnel to provide an interim government for Iraq. In order to accomplish this task, the White House assigned Katja Bullock to work as the human resources director for the CPA. Katja was responsible for filling the U.S. civilian positions required for the success of the CPA. In her regular job, Katja was a special assistant to the president of the United States for Human Resources. Katja Bullock, to the best of my recollection, had two stints of service in Baghdad. Each was for a couple of months. I met her during her second tour in Iraq when she signed up to participate in a trip I organized for the members of the CPA. Following the trip, I had the opportunity to speak with Katja on a couple of occasions, including her last evening in Baghdad prior to her return to Washington, D.C.

Toward the end of our conversation she asked, "Frank, is there anything you want me to tell the president?"

I must admit I was agog. "You," I responded (it was a question more than a statement), "will be speaking with the president?"

"Yes," she said. "I report to him regularly. The last time I returned to Washington, he called me into his office and had me tell him all about my time in Baghdad."

To that I responded, "First of all Katja, I want you to know that I don't tell the president anything . . . he tells me! Nevertheless, I do have one question I'd like you to ask him." I then went on to ask a question I believed contained information of which the president needed to be aware. He may already have had the information I was presenting in my question, but since I had a direct line to him, I took the opportunity to give Katja my question. (I will discuss my question to Katja for the president at length in a subsequent chapter.)

At the end of our conversation, Katja said, "Frank, when you return to the U.S. you'll have to come to the White House and have lunch with me."

In retrospect, I believe that I would have had any number of questions for Katja Bullock to present to President George W. Bush given the insights I have today. Had I to do it over again, the questions I would now ask are whether or not my observations about U.S. strategy in the Global War on Terrorism are accurate. Does the United States have a strategic plan in the GWOT, or am I seeing things that aren't there?

I am convinced that the United States has at least three strategic objectives in the Global War on Terrorism. These objectives are not necessarily obvious to the American public and are not clearly articulated by the present administration. Yet I believe that our strategic goals are self-evident and motivate our continued presence in Iraq. (I am here only considering the strategic objectives as they relate to Iraq and not the larger strategic implications contained in the phrase "axis of evil.") I believe that our national debate pertaining to our continued presence in Iraq needs to explore the strategic implications inherent in a global war on terrorism.

The first strategic objective of the United States in the Global War on Terrorism, as it seems self-evident to me, is to fight that war on foreign soil and not on the streets of our cities. The purpose of this first strategic objective is to prevent any more 9/11s from occurring within our country. We desire to conduct our operations in someone else's "back yard." It is no accident that Iraq has become the magnet for Arab terrorism. Every self-respecting terrorist who opposes us wants to go to Iraq (not the United States), find U.S. military and civilian personnel, and exterminate them. While I was in Baghdad, it was common knowledge that Saddam's former presidential palace and home of the CPA was the second-most important target for terrorist attacks in the world . . . second only to the White House. We were constantly in the news because of attacks directed against us. The Green Zone was continually under fire from mortars and rockets that fell indiscriminately within it. Entrances into the Green Zone were customarily the focus of suicide bombers and other attacks. Physical security was the most significant issue for all of us deployed to Baghdad.

In order to enhance security for those of us living on the grounds of the former presidential palace, a "big voice" was installed. A big voice is a loudspeaker system with a voice that sounds as if it is digitally produced. It can be heard up to a mile away. Warning messages were broadcast over the big voice to assist in providing security for the personnel assigned to the CPA. The scenario generally went like this: A rocket or mortar would explode, and a blast from the concussion could sometimes be felt throughout the Green Zone. Immediately following the explosion the big voice would bellow, "Take cover!" "Take cover!" It sounded particularly eerie during the night and reminded me of the big voice at Khobar towers in Saudi Arabia during the first Gulf War.

The only drawback to the big voice is that it was not part of an early warning alert system. A rocket would be heard overhead; there would be an explosion, and only then was a warning given. Rocket, explosion, WARNING! Well that's helpful! How about rocket, WARNING, explosion?

I remember being shaken and awakened at 0200 hours one day when a rocket landed not too far away from my hooch (i.e., containerized living compartment). The big voice came on: "Take cover!" "Take cover!" I rolled over in bed and pulled my covers over my head. That was my idea of taking cover in the middle of the night! Hey, tell me before it goes off, not afterward!

The first strategic objective of the United States in the Global War on Terrorism is to fight that war outside of our country.

The second strategic objective of the United States, in my opinion, is to plant a democracy in that part of the world that spawns terror. History demonstrates that democracies do not tend to go to war against other democracies. Our second strategic objective is to transform Southwest Asia and the Middle East through the introduction of democratic states. I seriously doubt that this objective will ever be overtly stated as part of our foreign policy. The reasons for this are manifold. The most obvious reason for keeping silent regarding this strategic objective is that our Arab partners in the region are not democratic states. They would undoubtedly react vehemently against any stated ambition of the United States to establish and perpetuate democracy throughout the region. It would not surprise me to learn that this aspect of our strategic plan precipitated the search for a *cause celèbre* for the invasion of Iraq. In other words, the United States did not invade Iraq over the issue of weapons of mass destruction (WMD). We invaded Iraq because that action was integral to our strategic goals as a nation in combating terrorism. The WMD issue gave the United States a plausible justification for exercising our strategic objectives.

The debate in which the American public might want to become involved vis-à-vis our strategy in the Global War on Terrorism is how much we are willing to invest as a nation in the establishment and perpetuation of democracy throughout the world. I find it telling that we already seem to be tired of our engagement in Iraq. We've grown weary of the cost of the war and of American loss of life in Iraq. And we've grown impatient with the Iraqi people as they establish democratic institutions and policies. It may be that our "tactical expenses" do not justify our "strategic objectives," but this is not a discussion that we have entertained.

As an aside, I wondered how much the American Revolution cost the King of France. It was certainly a strategic objective of the French king to degrade the power, prestige, and influence of England in the world. And it was to that end that the resources of France were invested to assist us in gaining our independence. The surrender of the British at Yorktown was only made possible by the arrival of the French fleet. Without the support of the French, one could well argue that the United States would not have achieved independence in the eighteenth century. The fact of the matter is that as many as ten thousand French personnel died as a result of the American Revolution. Most of these, to be clear, died of disease rather than armed conflict. The long-term economic impact on the French treasury appears to have been national bankruptcy. How much is the United States willing to expend in the establishment and perpetuation of democracy in Iraq? Is the establishment of democracy in Iraq in the best interest of U.S. strategic objectives?

Strategic thinkers must consider the staggering cost of our continued presence in Iraq juxtaposed to what it might cost the United States to conduct the war against terrorism on our streets. What would it cost us as a nation, not only in terms of economics, to have one or two 9/11-type events occurring each month within our borders?

The third objective that I discern in our Global War on Terrorism in Iraq can only be understood by pondering a map of the world. Regardless of our stated reasons for invading Iraq, its strategic import cannot be minimized. With one fell swoop the United States accomplished two crucial tasks in the Global War on Terrorism. In the first place, we isolated Syria. The isolation of Syria is strategically significant because Syria, along with Iran, is an exporter of international terrorism. When one looks at a map of Syria with its neighbors, the invasion of Iraq becomes crystal clear. Syria has become encircled by nations friendly to the United States. Turkey, our NATO partner and friend, borders Syria to the north. Iraq, a rising democratic state, borders Syria to the east and southeast. Jordan, with whom the United States has enjoyed good relations for years, borders Syria to the south. Israel and Lebanon complete the encirclement of Syria.

Another obvious conclusion can be drawn from looking at a map of the Middle East and Southwest Asia. The introduction of democracy in Iraq has the potential of influencing the establishment of democracy in neighboring Iran. The younger generation in Iran is already strongly influenced by American music and fashion. Some observers believe that, left to its own devices, Iran will transform itself into a democratic state in due course. A free and prosperous Iraq might tip the scales for democracy in Iran.

Finally, there is the effect that the invasion of Iraq may have on the Kingdom of Saudi Arabia. Islamic militancy in much of the Arab world is an outgrowth of Wahhabism. Wahhabism is the very strict and conservative brand of the Muslim faith practiced in Saudi Arabia that has been the driving influence of Islamic terrorism in our world. By invading Iraq, the United States has placed Saudi Arabia on notice. They may be our good friends in the region, but we will not sit idly by and watch as their "sons" crash airplanes into our skyscrapers. If Saudi Arabia will not clean up its own mess, we will!

I am not convinced that the invasion of Iraq was an accidental incursion based upon flawed information regarding the weapons of mass destruction. It is a carefully calculated strategic plan for surrounding Syria with nations belligerent to it and friendly to the United States. Moreover, the invasion of Iraq places a democratic state next door to Iran and Saudi Arabia so as to influence the future development and history of those nations. Iraq was a carefully chosen relatively secular Arab state that has strategic import for the United States in that region. It is the cornerstone of the domino theory in reverse. These strategic objectives of the United States may be obscure in our national debate, but they have not been lost on the Syrians, the Iranians, or Arab terror organizations!

The Global War on Terrorism is not merely a slogan. It is a carefully considered strategy to transform the geopolitical face of the world. Our strategic plan has at least three aspects to it that I can discern. First, the war is not to be fought on U.S. soil. Second, the aim of the war is to establish a democratic state in the part of the world that spawns and supports terrorism. Finally, the purpose of this war is to isolate Syria from any potential allies in the region and influence the political and social development of both Iran and Saudi Arabia.

Or am I just imaging a strategy that does not exist?

I returned from Baghdad in May of 2004 after twelve and a half months in Iraq. In July, I called Katja Bullock and took her up on her offer to have lunch at the White House Mess. The mess is located in the bowels of the White House and is managed and operated by the U.S. Navy. It is a small dining room with about a dozen tables capable of seating forty or fifty people. Guests are waited on by personnel wearing white waistcoats and eat from plates with the presidential seal. Eating at the White House Mess was truly a wonderful adventure in fine dining. It is something that I would never have imagined doing in my wildest dreams. Just as we were about to have dessert, I noticed Dan Senor seated at a table across the room. Dan served as the spokesperson for Ambassador Bremer and the CPA. Katja and I waved to him and he walked over to our table and extended greetings to us. After Dan walked away, Katja informed me that he was a skilled spokesperson because he was always able to respond to questions asked of him with the agenda of Ambassador Bremer and the CPA rather than the agenda of those asking questions. That comment by Katja was definitely worth the price of admission to the White House Mess. We don't have to respond to others on their terms; we can respond on our terms with our own agendas. I made up my mind to file that tidbit away for future reference.

I am not an individual who aspires to greatness or renown. I do not see myself as a person of note. But I do see my life and everyone else's life as a wonderful adventure with a myriad of unique experiences. So, what is the chance that one would get invited to the White House Mess for lunch and then while dining bump into someone known to him or her?

After eating, one is permitted to keep one's menu as a souvenir. It is an eight-and-a-half-by-eleven-inch piece of navy blue card stock with gold lettering and a gold tassel holding the interior white page with the menu. On the front of the menu, there is the presidential seal surrounded by stars. The reverse side has the history of the White House Mess, ending with the awards given to the men and women of the Navy who have served in the White House. They have received the Joint Meritorious Unit Award with oak leaf cluster, the Navy Meritorious Unit Commendation, and the Army Meritorious Unit Commendation. One is also given a box of M&Ms with the presidential seal. Imagine that—presidential M&Ms!

I am troubled by our national response to the war in Iraq. No, I am not troubled that many if not most American citizens want to leave Iraq because of the cost of American lives and the expenditure of American dollars. I am troubled because it appears that many of the individuals who wear the burden and mantle of responsibility for political leadership in our country want to make strategic decisions based upon tactical information. The leaders of our nation must be engaged in a debate about the big picture and not about the day-to-day vicissitudes of tactical mission planning and execution. I believe that the people of our nation have the maturity and intellectual ability to grasp the intricacies of our strategic goals and objectives. And if given the opportunity, they will weigh in on our aims as a nation and help set the direction for world involvement.

"Katja, I don't tell the president anything . . . he tells me. But I do have a couple of questions for him. I'd like to know if I'm correct in my observations about the Global War on Terrorism. Is it our objective to fight this war on foreign soil? Is it our intention to democratize Southwest Asia and the Middle East? And was the invasion of Iraq a geopolitical incursion aimed at isolating Syria and influencing the political and social development Iran and Saudi Arabia? Or, am I just imaging things by thinking that we are engage in a global war with a global strategy?"

Chapter 2

The Right Reverend George Packard

I have often been asked by clergy in the Episcopal Church to explain my job as a chaplain in the U.S. Army. During the years that I served as the command chaplain for the 94th Regional Readiness Command at Ft. Devens, Massachusetts, it was easy to answer their question. I stated simply that I was the Army Reserve bishop of New England. This was an apt description of the scope and duties of my position as the command chaplain. Furthermore, I had a staff of two other chaplains and four chaplain assistants to help me in carrying out the religious support mission in New England. My job was very much akin to that of a bishop with a diocesan staff.

The liturgy for the ordination of a bishop in the Episcopal *Book of Common Prayer* explains the Episcopal Church's theology regarding the primary duty and responsibility of a bishop. Representatives of the diocese standing before the presiding bishop say the following, "N., Bishop in the Church of God, the clergy and people of the Diocese of N., trusting in the guidance of the Holy Spirit, have chosen N.N. to be a bishop and chief pastor." The first and foremost duty of a bishop in the Episcopal Church is to be the "chief pastor." Now, I am not a bishop and was not ordained to the bishopric by the Army. I did, however, determine to become a faithful chief pastor for the command in which I served. I established my primary goal as that of providing spiritual care to the caregivers (i.e., taking good care of subordinate chaplains and chaplain assistants) whom I served as their supervisor.

One of the first lessons of military service is not to do anything or go anywhere without orders. Military personnel go where they are ordered to go and not where they choose to go.

I was sitting at a staff meeting of the Coalition Provisional Authority during my first month in Baghdad. A CPA staff member walked in a bit late. He excused himself for his tardiness and then explained that he had gotten caught up in a situation at the front gate. A young Marine reservist had just shown up who wanted to join the fight in Iraq. He had been sitting at home watching the events unfold on television. He packed his gear into his duffel bags, bought a plane ticket to Jordan, hired a car, and drove to Baghdad. He had just arrived and wanted to know how to "marry up" with the Marines. The actions of this Marine demonstrated a great deal of initiative, but he had to be sent home. He hadn't in-processed. He didn't have a medical screening—or a weapon, for that matter. Military personnel don't just show up to fight. They are ordered to duty. There have been occasions when I've waited at airports an hour before flight time for someone to arrive from my unit with travel orders. Orders not only command a person or unit to move, they also provide funding for travel and lodging. I have witnessed individuals who traveled prior to receiving orders and were not reimbursed for accommodations and rental cars. Orders authorize military personnel to move and then allocate monies to pay for that movement.

I received a phone call in October of 2002 from MSG (Master Sergeant) Dave Gagnon at MacDill Air Force Base, Tampa, Florida. He was serving in the CENTCOM chaplain's office and had been speaking with CH (COL) Gerry Robinson, Command Chaplain. CH Robinson was searching for someone to come to MacDill and serve as the deputy rear chaplain when the team was pushed forward to Camp Doha, Qatar. MSG Gagnon wanted to know if I'd be interested.

On the morning of 11 September 2001, I was on my way to serve as chaplain for a military funeral in Waltham, Massachusetts. The Mass Pike was awful as usual, and I was somewhat anxious about arriving in time for the ceremony even though I'd given myself plenty of lead time. I generally have my radio on, but for some strange reason I had it turned off. I was probably rehearsing the funeral service in my mind. I arrived at the cemetery and pulled up behind a vehicle from New York with the honor guard from Ft. Drum. The NCOIC (noncommissioned officer in charge) came over to my car, saluted, and asked if I had heard the news and what had just occurred at the World Trade Center. As he spoke, another soldier rushed over to the car and informed us that a second plane had just crashed into the other tower. Since I was already on orders, I went to my headquarters at Ft. Devens immediately following the funeral.

The weeks and months following the attack on the World Trade Center and the Pentagon were agonizing. I would fly out of airports and see the

National Guard troops on duty. I watched as U.S. forces fought in Afghanistan and listened to the news concerning Iraq. Here was the United States at war, and I wasn't doing a thing. Certainly I was in the Army Reserve, but that didn't seem enough to me.

MSG Gagnon's call was just what I'd wanted: an opportunity to serve the Army in a more meaningful way. I jumped at the chance to be part of the team at MacDill as they planned the invasion of Iraq. Nothing, however, came out of my conversation with MSG Gagnon. Filling the position got stuck in red tape. Toward the end of 2002, I received another phone call from MSG Gagnon. There was another position in the CENTCOM chaplain's office. Was I interested? Again, I jumped at the opportunity, and again nothing came of it. Then in February of 2003, I was contacted a third time and asked if I was still interested in serving at MacDill. I was assured that everything would go smoothly this time and I'd be there by the end of the month. The date slipped, and I was given a new report date of mid-March for in-processing at Ft. Benning, Georgia. I was also informed that although my orders weren't "cut" yet, I could pick them up at USARC (U.S. Army Reserve Command) in Atlanta on my way to Ft. Benning. The mobilization was so locked in and a certainty that I forgot one of the first rules of military service. Don't go anywhere without orders . . . don't even pick them up on the way!

I had resigned my position as rector of St. Michael's-on-the-Heights in Worcester, Massachusetts, and headed off to Ft. Benning. I resigned from the parish because the orders I was to pick up at USARC could keep me deployed for two years. I had driven as far as Fredericksburg, Virginia, when I got a phone call from the USARC chaplain's office. Where was I, they wanted to know. I explained that I was on my way to Georgia to pick up my orders and report to the MOB (mobilization) station. The individual with whom I was speaking then said, "Pull off the highway so we can talk." I pulled over to the shoulder of the road and listened as I was informed that the Army did not have a job for me and to turn around and go home. My heart sank. I was out of work with no job prospects!

I immediately began calling people to inform them of what had taken place. I also called the Canon to the Ordinary in the Diocese of Western Massachusetts to see if there might be any work in the diocese for me. She promised to get back to me later in the day. When she called back, she said, "Frank, come on home. We are going to have you work in the diocesan office until we find something for you. We'll pay you your entire stipend and allowances."

You could have knocked me over with a feather. It was the finest treatment I have ever received as a priest in the Episcopal Church. It was also the most humbling thing that has ever happened to me in my life. It was evident that my bishop, the Rt. Rev. Gordon Scruton, understood the primary responsibility of a bishop. He was fulfilling his role as the chief pastor, and he was providing care to the caregiver. He was and is a great blessing in my life.

The events that had taken place over the previous six months were ridiculous, and I had been treated shamefully by the Army. On three separate occasions I had been geared up for mobilization and then had the rug pulled out from under my feet at the last moment. I wrote a letter and copied the Army Chief of Chaplains, my two-star commander, my diocesan bishop, the Episcopal Bishop for Chaplaincies, and the USARC command chaplain. In it I detailed the entire series of events that had brought me to this place. I ended the letter by stating, "I am in shock and awe!" Two days later I received my orders to report to Ft. Benning and then on to MacDill A.F.B.

I had wanted to serve our country in a more active way than fulfilling my reserve commitment. I now had orders in hand to join the team that was engaged in combat operations in Iraq. The only question remaining was, "How might I parlay these orders into service in Iraq rather than Tampa, Florida?"

✠

Life at a mobilization station is unpleasant. The billeting arrangements are substandard, and the food is terrible. One is herded everywhere, and then there are long lines to stand in all day long. The secret to mobilization and demobilization is bringing a book to read. The other secret about going to the MOB site is to be certain that one's immunizations are all up to date. Eleven shots are required for deployment to Iraq, Afghanistan, and Kuwait. I needed three shots, but many soldiers need five or six. Some need them all—ouch! I counted up the total of all the shots I've received over my twenty-five-year Army career: seventy. Most of them are your average everyday variety of shots like tetanus, hepatitis, and typhoid. Then there are what I call the "romantic" shots I've received, like anthrax, the plague, yellow fever, and cholera. The standing joke among soldiers regarding all their shots is that they ought to glow in the dark when the lights are turned off. I ought to be a neon sign! I've also been required to take choloroquin when deployed on a number of occasions. The only drawback regarding the use of choloroquin is that one may not be a blood donor for three years following its use.

The good thing about my mobilization at Ft. Benning is that I received an e-mail from CH Robinson at CENTCOM informing me that I would be going forward with a new organization that was being established to rebuild Iraq following the war. He believed that my background and expertise in civil military operations made me the perfect choice to serve as a chaplain on this team. I would be going to Baghdad a couple of days after reporting to MacDill A.F.B. I was thrilled. I had gotten my most fervent wish and heart's desire.

✣

The wonderful thing about being an Episcopal priest is that no matter where in the world one ends up, the church is present. Equally important is the knowledge that a bishop of the church will be present to provide pastoral oversight. The Episcopal or Anglican Church was present in Haiti, Saudi Arabia, Iraq, and Kuwait during my deployments to each of those countries. The Rev. Andrew White would explain to me a few months after my arrival in Iraq that St. George's Church in Baghdad was part of the Diocese of Cyprus and the Gulf and that the Bishop of the diocese was Clive Handford. Bishop Handford had served the congregation in Baghdad many years earlier as their vicar. Andrew was also the person who would keep me informed about Bishop Handford's itinerary and possible visit to Baghdad. I requested that Andrew ask the bishop if he would be willing to come to the palace and preside at our 0730 hours service when he did visit the city. The bishop agreed and then visited our little congregation on two occasions during my year there. The thing I noticed about our congregation at the palace in Baghdad was that it was no different from congregations everywhere else: when the bishop appears, worship attendance increases!

Bishop Handford is a most engaging and friendly fellow. He was extremely supportive of me and cared a great deal about my work at the palace and at St. George's. I was fortunate to serve as Bishop and Mrs. Handford's host when they attended the Episcopal Church's General Convention in 2006. I was even more fortunate to see him again at the institution of a new vicar at the Anglican parish in Kuwait City.

✣

The bishop for chaplaincies in the Episcopal Church is George Packard. His office used to be called the Office of the Bishop for the Armed Forces (OBAF). Bishop Packard's sphere of responsibility has increased greatly in recent years. What I notice about Bishop Packard is that he has a wonderful vision for the ministry of chaplains. I also notice that he is a wonderful pastor to chaplains on active duty in the military and those called to active duty from the National Guard or Army Reserve.

I was the senior Episcopal chaplain in Iraq during my tour there. That meant that I became keenly aware of the needs and concerns of the other

Episcopal chaplains in theater. Were it not for Bishop Packard, many of these chaplains would have not received any pastoral support at all.

A suicide bomber entered a dining facility on 21 December 2004 in Mosul, Iraq. The result was that fourteen U.S. service members, four U.S. contractors, and three Iraqi military personnel were killed. In addition, sixty-nine people were wounded, including forty-four U.S. military personnel. One of the wounded was an Episcopal priest called to active duty from the National Guard. As a result of the attack, this priest spent a year in the hospital and at home recovering from his wounds. According to him, his own bishop never came to visit him during his year recovery. It is troubling to me to learn that any priest in our church does not believe that his or her bishop is a "chief pastor," let alone one who is hospitalized for injuries suffered in combat. If it were not for Bishop Packard, this priest would not have received any pastoral support whatsoever from a "chief pastor."

Bishop Packard has such great concern for his chaplains that he visited Baghdad during Lent of 2004. He came to Baghdad as the guest of Bishop Clive Handford and joined the palace congregation on Sunday morning. It was a spectacular service. Two bishops of the church had placed themselves in harm's way to come to Baghdad and serve as "chief pastor" to their congregation there. Bishop Packard spent a couple of days with us and led a quiet day for his priests deployed to Iraq. It was because of this quiet day that I was about to learn something else perplexing.

What I learned is that not all chaplains deployed to the theater of operations in Iraq, Afghanistan, and Kuwait enjoy the same pastoral support that I receive from both my diocesan bishop and the bishop for chaplaincies. I actually ran across three Episcopal chaplains from the same diocese whose bishop could care less that they had been deployed to a combat zone. One of these chaplains sought to engage his bishop upon his return from a second deployment to Iraq and was told that they had nothing to discuss until such time as his parish assessment was up to date! I would suggest that the words of the presentation on page 513 of the Book of Common Prayer is worthy of reflection on a regular basis by those who are in the process of selecting a "chief pastor" to serve Christ's flock: "N., Bishop in the Church of God, the clergy and people of the Diocese of N., trusting in the guidance of the Holy Spirit have chosen N.N. to be a bishop and chief pastor. We therefore ask you to lay your hands upon *him* and in the power of the Holy Spirit to consecrate *him* a bishop in the one, holy, catholic, and apostolic Church."

I spent a little more than a year recruiting a Roman Catholic priest for the Army Reserve. I had him slated to deploy with an M.P. battalion going to Iraq following the completion of his basic chaplain schooling. While he was at chaplain school, however, the Active Component (active duty soldiers) grabbed him and sent him to Ft. Leonard Wood (or, as we refer to it, Fort Lost-in-the-Woods), Missouri. The greater needs of the Army always take precedence in situations such as this, however. To replace him, they sent the unit a brand-new chaplain, a first lieutenant. He seemed like an OK fellow even though he was a bit strange. For example, he decided to go out one day and buy twenty-four cases of wine. Although he was a Baptist clergyman, he wanted to make certain that the Roman Catholics had ample wine for their services while deployed. That was rather thoughtful, even though a bit excessive. One day this chaplain called me and asked if I could give him the name of a Roman Catholic priest. He wanted to have the twenty-four cases of wine consecrated before they deployed to Iraq so they would be ready to go once they arrived. I informed him that no priest was going to consecrate twenty-four cases of wine for his upcoming year in Iraq, but I did give him the name of a Roman Catholic chaplain to contact. You might well imagine the phone call I received from this priest following his conversation with the Baptist chaplain.

I decided that it would be worth a trip to Ft. Dix, New Jersey, to see how this unit and chaplain were doing at their mobilization station. It turned out to be fortuitous that I went to visit them. A night or two earlier this chaplain had gotten up to go to the bathroom at 0230 hours. When he returned, he began jumping up and down on his bunk screaming that he believed in Satan and worshipped the devil. His roommates became more than a little concerned and reported what had happened to their commander. She, in turn, reported this to me. I was also to learn that this chaplain had taken a young soldier aside and asked if he could have the young man's MP3 player if he was killed in combat! I took the chaplain aside and learned that he had been offered a full-time Army position in the United States and didn't really want to get deployed. I came to the conclusion that this was the reason for his aberrant behavior. I was determined, however, not to permit him to act "crazy" to avoid deployment and then get a full-time Army job in the United States. I saw to it that he received a psychological evaluation. He was then given the opportunity to resign his commission. It was an opportunity he couldn't pass up!

Soldiers going into harm's way need caregivers who are healthy and well adjusted. They don't need to have chaplains who qualify for the India, Delta, Ten, Tango designator. What's that? Well, . . .

The military uses a phonetic alphabet in order to conduct operations without error. A=Alpha, B=Bravo, and so on. If I am speaking with someone in the military who asks me to spell my last name, I respond, "Wismer: I spell Whisky, India, Sierra, Mike, Echo, Romeo."

A designator or skill identifier is a special classification given to military personnel. These designators may be given to indicate advanced military schooling or special training of some sort. The India, Delta, Ten, Tango designator suggests, therefore, that one is an ID10T.

I would never deploy a chaplain that required more counseling than he or she could provide. Religious support to personnel in a combat theater is dangerous and demanding. It is important that we deploy only the best chaplains down range with America's sons and daughters. It is equally important to me that we provide quality care to these caregivers.

Chapter 3

Major Keith June

U.S. Army

The most inappropriate sermon I ever heard preached in my life was on Easter Sunday of 2003 in Doha, Qatar. Doha was the forward headquarters for CENTCOM (Central Command) and was a beehive of activity in light of the fact that the invasion of Iraq was underway. I can best describe the U.S. base at Doha as a series of warehouses used for offices, dining, and sleeping accommodations. The curious thing about the warehouses used for offices is that within each one tents had been erected on metal frames to conduct the business of the command. The warehouses used for billeting boasted hundreds of connex containers stacked on two levels, with catwalks connecting them. The bathrooms in these warehouses were a sight to behold. Each probably had room for one hundred military personnel to use at a time.

I was at the base for three days in-processing, awaiting transportation to Kuwait, receiving my second in a series of six anthrax shots, and getting acquainted with the CENTCOM chaplain team forward. The base at Doha was a bleak way station in the desert with nothing much to commend it. It was hot during the day, and the air conditioning in the billeting warehouses made it too cold to sleep at night outside of one's sleeping bag. The base at Doha is now the location for U.S. military personnel stationed in Iraq, Afghanistan, and Kuwait to go on their four-day passes while in theater. Needless to say, I did not take advantage of this privilege during my second tour to Kuwait in 2006–2007. I can be just as miserable in the desert of Kuwait as I can be in the desert of Qatar!

The reason why the sermon I heard on Easter Sunday at Doha was so inappropriate was not because the preacher was unprepared. The sermon didn't miss the mark because the speaker hadn't carefully crafted his words or because he was a poor orator. It wasn't off target because it was boring or lacked powerful illustrations to assist in making the preacher's point. The sermon was atrocious because it was a theological nightmare. The theme this preacher had chosen and that he repeated time and time again was, "It's Friday, but Easter's coming!" I must admit I wanted to stand up and scream, "No dummy, you've missed the point entirely! It may have been Friday or Good Friday in our lives, but Easter has arrived, and we've been set free from that which imprisons us or torments our souls!" Had I not been seated in the middle of the auditorium, I would have quietly made my way to the door and departed. The preacher was preaching the crucifixion on Easter morning.

✣

The Army sent me to Vicenza, Italy, for three weeks in April of 2006 to support the 173rd Airborne during its reintegration process upon returning from a year in Afghanistan. While I was there, I was determined to attend all the services conducted at the post chapel. I went to Catholic mass, the contemporary Protestant service, and the traditional Protestant service. What I discovered is that the theology of Christian chaplains in the military is remarkably similar regardless of their denomination. That theology is summarized in the words of one of the chaplains at Vicenza, when during his sermon he turned around, faced the altar, pointed at the crucifix, and proclaimed, "It's all about the cross!"

It is *not* all about the cross! There were literally tens of thousands of people crucified by the Romans during the time of Jesus. There is only one we know about who came back from the dead. It is not all about the cross. Had Jesus simply died and not risen from the grave, there would be no Christianity. Moreover, we Christians do not worship on Friday the day of the crucifixion; we worship on Sunday, the day of the resurrection. It is not all about the cross! If it is all about one thing, it is about *resurrection*!

The life-giving message of Christianity for those about to go to war and for those just returning from combat is not that it is "just about the cross" or that "it's Friday, but Easter's coming." The salvific message of the Church for all combatants is that regardless of the trauma they have experienced or the pain they shall endure, there is always the promise of new life. Soldiers in a combat theater or on their way to war know what "Friday" looks like. They live with death and destruction. They are constantly in harm's way and risk injury daily. They understand the burden of the cross far better than any preacher. What they may not comprehend is that the promise of new life and resurrection is a present reality.

✣

I traveled to Kuwait on 23 April, flying Arab Emirates Air, and was met at KCIA (Kuwait City International Airport). I was then taken to the Hilton Kuwait to meet up with the Organization for Relief and Humanitarian Assistance (ORHA) under the leadership of Lieutenant General (retired) Garner. The ORHA Team had been selected months earlier and had begun planning back at the Pentagon to coordinate humanitarian and civic action in Iraq following the war. I was a late addition to the team and was joining them toward the end of their coordination efforts in Kuwait. I was tasked to provide "situational awareness" for the CENTCOM Chaplain regarding religious support to ORHA. Because the team was made up of senior military and civilian personnel, we did not get billeted in one of the "dust bowl" camps in the Kuwaiti desert. We lived in villas on the Persian Gulf that are part of the Hilton Hotel complex in Kuwait City. We had daily maid service and ate in the Hilton five-star restaurant. I thought I'd died and gone to Army heaven!

✠

Major Keith June (now a lieutenant colonel) served as a communications officer on the ORHA team. He had worked in the Pentagon, and it would be his responsibility to get communications up and running once the team got to Baghdad. Although MAJ June was not the senior communications officer, he was the one who provided stability to that staff section as other senior communications officers rotated in and out of Baghdad. Little did I realize at the time that MAJ June would end up playing a significant role in helping me establish a vibrant religious support program for U.S. military and civilian personnel assigned to ORHA. We were to become very good friends in Iraq and then cement our friendship later by spending a year together at Camp Arifjan, Kuwait, in 2006–2007, when he served as the Commander for the 54th Signal Battalion. Keith June is an outstanding, highly competent officer who I am firmly convinced is destined to become a general officer in the U.S. Army.

✠

The chapel at the palace in Baghdad was unlike any other that one might imagine. I was given Saddam's former "throne room" at the south end of the palace in which to conduct services; it was also to be used as a prayer area for Muslims. It was a huge room with a marble floor and marble-clad walls four or five stories high. The ceiling boasted an ornate chandelier, and at its center was a picture of the heavenly Jerusalem surrounded by eight horses representing the Prophet's ascent and descent there as described in the Qur'an. The room was so large that it was used to seat four hundred individuals for dinner in November of 2003 during the Marine Corps birthday celebration. A crew of three Iraqi day workers required two and a half days to change all the light bulbs in the room. Two large murals were centered on the eastern and western walls. The room would have reminded one of a section of St. Peter's Basilica in Rome had it not been for the fact that the mural on the eastern wall depicted a number of Scud missiles being launched in the direction of Jerusalem. Also, there were hundreds of decorative symbols on the walls and ceiling containing the Arabic initials of Saddam Hussein. The "pews" were palace furniture consisting of sofas and chairs clad in green satin upholstery with gold-colored armrests, legs, and backboards. *Gaudy* would be an apt word to describe them.

A French reporter had filed a story for a French publication taking umbrage with the way in which the "chapel" had been set up. He complained that the Christians had taken the majority of the space in this room and the Muslims, whose country and palace this was, had only been given a small space to conduct their prayers. I was shown a copy of the article following its publication and was somewhat dismayed by the portrayal of the "ugly American" through the division of the worship space in the chapel. Apparently the writer had no interest in researching the fact that the prayer rug used in the chapel for Muslim prayer was more than fifty feet long, thirty feet wide, and woven completely of silk. It had been recovered from the palace storage warehouse and was valued at more than twenty-five thousand dollars. In selecting it from the storage area, I had suggested that it was the most suitable rug because only the best should be given to the Iraqis for the worship of Allah. The altar that we used for Christian worship was an old desk covered with an extra tablecloth from the dining facility. While cursory examination of the chapel might have led one to surmise that the Muslims were being treated as the second-class citizens of the worship area, nothing could have been further from the truth.

✢

One of the requirements for Army personnel is that they pass a physical training test twice a year. That test consists of push-ups, sit-ups, and a two-mile run. The test sets differing standards for the number of repetitions to be completed and the time in which the run is finished based upon the age and sex of the soldier. To remain physically fit during my tour in Baghdad, I got into the habit of running four miles daily. I had established a course in the Green Zone winding through the streets toward the Assassins Gate (so named because snipers had been situated there during the fight for Baghdad) and then returning to the palace. Over time, others began joining me for this daily adventure, which became known as the "chaplain's death run." This was so named by MAJ June in light of the fact that we ran daily at noon—even through the summer months, when temperatures reach 140 degrees. Our running group grew to as many as a dozen individuals at one point during my time in Baghdad. The Monday run was always the sermon discussion run from the previous day. I was intrigued by the fact that a group of senior Army officers along with a couple of civilian contractors wanted to carry on a weekly theological discussion during our Monday jaunt around the Green Zone. There were also many times during the middle of the week when the conversation during our runs would turn to the upcoming Sunday's readings and possible themes for preaching. My running partners were never shy about suggesting topics for my sermons. Generally it was MAJ June who began the theological dialogue. I began to find that I looked forward to our daily runs because they stimulated my reflection on the Scriptures. I must admit, however, that my favorite part of the run was when we returned to the palace grounds and jumped into the swimming pool located out back.

✢

The swimming pool at the palace was beautiful. It was situated beside a cabana and a pavilion. It was larger than an Olympic-sized pool, and at the deep end was a springboard and a high platform for diving. The 82nd Airborne chaplains used the palace and the pool area as an R&R location for their troops. It was customary for groups of twenty or thirty soldiers from the 82nd to spend a day at the palace. They'd tour the place, have lunch in the dining facility, and then lie beside the pool and go for a swim.

One afternoon when we had completed our run, I was drying off in the sun after having jumped into the pool. Near me were five soldiers from the 82nd who were having a day at the palace. I overheard them egging one soldier on.

"I bet you haven't got the nerve to do a belly flop off the platform," one said.

"How much willya give me if I do?" he responded.

"Twenty bucks," came the reply.

"I'm not doing that for twenty bucks!"

This conversation went on and on until the bet reached two hundred dollars. "OK, I'll do it," the soldier assured them.

I was thinking to myself that this is an accident waiting to happen. I also figured that one of us would be running to the medic's office just inside the rear of the palace for help at any moment.

The soldier got up, climbed the ladder to the high platform, surveyed the task at hand, and hurled himself, spread eagle, toward the water. THWAP! He hit the water with a slap, and when he surfaced from his "dive," he was groaning.

His belly was pink, along with his legs, arms, and face. Not to be outdone, his buddies all decided that if he could do it, they could do it. Each of them in turn hit the water with a slap. I guess if you haven't got an airplane to jump out of this is the next best thing!

✠

Not only was the chapel at Saddam's former palace unlike anything one might imagine, so was the congregation. Across the hall from the chapel was the dining facility. There were rules governing entrance into the dining area, including one that prohibited weapons from being brought into it. This was not the case for the chapel. Everyone was invited into the chapel as they were. It was commonplace to look out into the congregation to find soldiers and marines clad in body armor with Kevlar helmets resting beside them. It was also the rule rather than the exception to see dozens and dozens of worshippers with holsters and 9mm pistols attached to their belts. Leaning against the pews were rifles, and under the pews one could sometimes spy a crew-served (requiring more that one person to operate) machine gun with bandoleer. It reminded me of a tidbit of history I'd come across while serving a congregation in Delaware. Shortly before the American Revolution, a group of soldiers from the Delaware Militia were attending divine services at the Anglican Church in Middletown. The vicar was a royalist and during the service prayed for the King of England. That led the members of the militia to rattle their muskets in response to the vicar's prayer. It turned out to be the last service conducted by that clergyman at St. Anne's Church. I figured I'd better watch what I said!

✠

During my tenure at Camp Arifjan, Kuwait, in 2007, I determined to prepare a Lenten meditation guide for all of the military and civilian personnel stationed there. I decided that I would invite thirty-nine other people to provide a short meditation based on a verse from Scripture that I had selected. The first person I asked was LTC Keith June. As it turned out, a couple of the people who had agreed to write meditations failed to do so, so Keith ended up writing more than one. It was interesting to have U.S. military personnel share with one another their reflections as we journeyed through Lent. It was noteworthy that my commander, Major General Thomas Robinson, agreed to write the meditation for Ash Wednesday.

Lieutenant Colonel Keith June wrote the following:

Monday: 05 March

Scriptural Reference: Matthew 5:5 "Blessed are the meek, for they shall inherit the earth."

Meditation:
As I read this passage many things came to mind. The beatitudes are some of the most beautiful and thought-provoking passages in the Bible. However, to be truthful, I have struggled with this passage, in part, because I didn't understand the word "meek."

Webster's dictionary defines meek as, "enduring injury with patience and without resentment."

What does it mean to be meek? Does it mean to be weak? Does it mean to be powerless?

Are the meek powerless or simply patient?

As I've grown older (and hopefully wiser), I've come to realize that the greatest strength and the most powerful people I've met are the meek. They have fought and won, at least to some extent, the greatest struggle of all, the great battle against oneself—the battle for self-discipline and self-control.

Every day I ask God for patience. We live in an age defined by speed. Everything must be done now! Our microwave society mandates that everything move at *our* speed. But the reality of the world is that we move at God's speed. God's time not our time. Life has taught me that it truly is *God's will*, not my will.

I've encountered many storms in the great walk called life. Sometimes things move much faster than I would like, but normally they move much slower than I would like. But above all, I've learned to deal with each situation, each problem, each challenge as a small blessing, a small gift from God. And as I live each day, I know that my life moves according to *God's plan*, not my plan.

So, are the meek the weak or the most powerful? Lent is a wonderful time to welcome meekness, to slow down and look for God's grace and presence. And if we can live our lives with patience, with love, "with enduring injury with patience and without resentment," then perhaps, we can inherit the earth.

LTC Keith June, 54th SIG BN[1]

✠

The first Sunday that I led worship services in Baghdad a total of twenty-three people attended. When I departed Iraq a little more than a year later, more than seven hundred and fifty people on average were praying or worshipping in the chapel weekly. I have discovered during my years of service in a combat theater of operations that the closer one gets to the fight, the higher the chapel attendance. I don't know if this is because "there are no atheists in foxholes" or because Operation Iraqi Freedom was conducted in the Garden of Eden. There is a case to be made for the impact that living on holy ground makes upon one. We lived adjacent to the Tigris River not far from the biblical Eden. We traveled to Babylon, Ur, and Nineveh. We weren't far from Ezekiel's tomb. I think that it is impossible to live on holy ground and not have it impact one's thinking and one's actions.

In retrospect, perhaps I needn't get too wrapped around the axle over the Easter Sunday sermon that I heard delivered in Doha. Perhaps the influence of living on holy ground is far greater than anyone can comprehend or imagine. Perhaps the voice of God speaks much more loudly than any preacher's sermon. Maybe I need to ponder MAJ June's meditation a little more thoroughly.

LTC Keith June and I ate lunch together every Sunday during the year we served together in Kuwait. I think that he would probably tell you that I was his spiritual mentor in the desert. I would tell you that he was mine.

Keith attended a black Southern Baptist church in South Carolina while growing up. Like me, he was aided by a very devout mother in his Christian development. While we were in Kuwait, Keith called home on one occasion, and his mother asked him if he was still a faithful churchgoer. He hesitated somewhat because he was attending the service that I was leading on Sundays and not attending the gospel service at Camp Arifjan. When he didn't answer her right away, she exclaimed, "You haven't become a Muslim, have you?" Apparently, Keith's mother has a friend whose children had also been in the Arab world and one of them had converted to Islam.

"No, mother," he responded. "Worse than that, I've become an Episcopalian!"

Chapter 4

Colonel Mike Scotto

U.S. Army Reserve

I am convinced that one day the national revenue of Iraq will be measured not in oil but in tourism. I believe that tourism could replace oil as the primary source of revenue for the Iraqi people. Three of the great religions of the world, Judaism, Christianity, and Islam, have their historic roots planted in Iraq. Iraq is home to the Garden of Eden. The Tigris and Euphrates Rivers are two of the four rivers mentioned in the Book of Genesis to help pinpoint the Garden of Eden. These two rivers flow through Iraq and empty into the Persian Gulf. A stable and peaceful Iraq with the infrastructure to support tourism could bring millions of sightseers to the country each year. The key is a peaceful and stable Iraq.

We began our thirteen-hour trek through the desert from Kuwait City to Baghdad in a caravan of thirty nontactical vehicles (i.e., SUVs) divided into three groups of ten each. The word "desolate" does not begin to capture the harshness of the landscape or do justice to the barrenness of the vast, brown desert sea. It is an endless void of hard-baked earth, windswept in places by clouds of dust. Yet in the midst of this wasteland people somehow survive.

I remember spying a hovel off to the left of our vehicle in the middle of nowhere. The baked mud hut had no roof. It had an opening for a door and a window, but nothing filled these openings. As we drove past, an Arab woman and two children emerged from the hut. I could hardly believe my eyes. How could anyone live in this desolate place with no visible means of survival? There was no oasis with water to drink. Because there was no water there were no crops. There were no animals anywhere in sight that might provide milk and meat. All that was visible was the drab brown desert floor, the hut, and the dust-filled wind. It dawned on me for the first time in my life that the biblical story of the fall of Adam and Eve and their expulsion from the Garden of Eden was not merely a theological conundrum. It was a story of survival. It was a tale of the survival of the cursed, and it was being played out again and again by the people we passed as we drove north!

✝

Ur, the home of Abraham (Ibrahim to the Muslims) is located in the south of Iraq. Visitors to Ur are taken to the ziggurat and to what is believed to be Abraham's home. The U.S. Army has a base of operations located near Ur. Military personnel on convoy use the base as a rest stop on their way to and from Kuwait. It was not an option for us to stop at Ur on our journey. Had I planned the trip, Ur would have been a "must see." Our little caravan did stop on two occasions. I am not exactly certain where we were, but it was above Ur and south of Baghdad. We pulled off the road because we were "lost." Actually, we never get "lost" in the Army. Soldiers don't get "lost." We were simply disoriented! Two of our vehicles headed off to find someone who could show us the route to Baghdad while the rest of us got out of the vehicles and stretched. It only took a matter of moments before children looking for money, an MRE (meal, ready to eat), candies, or water surrounded us.

One teenager approached me and handed me an envelope. I hesitated to take it for a moment because I had no idea what might be inside it. Was this a "letter bomb" from some Iraqi who hated Americans? All I could tell is that the writing on the envelope was in Arabic. The teenager ran off and returned with a middle-aged gentleman who spoke enough English to ask me to give it to the authorities. I took the envelope and began asking the members of our caravan if anyone could read Arabic. Luckily enough, we had someone with us who worked for the U.S. State Department and was fluent in Arabic. I handed the envelope to him, asked him what it might be, and requested that he turn it over to the authorities when we reached Baghdad. The envelope didn't contain a bomb, but more of a "bombshell." The message provided information and directions to a mass grave not far away from the little village where we stopped to rest. Iraqi troops had murdered dozens of Kuwaitis near there. During Iraq's invasion of Kuwait, the military rounded up prominent Kuwaitis, drove them north into the desert of Iraq and disposed of them. The good fellow who asked me pass the note on to the authorities wanted to make certain that these missing souls were found and their families informed.

✝

We had been traveling through the desert most of the day when the scenery finally changed. The bleak brown wasteland changed into an immense oasis.

We were surrounded by palm trees . . . date palm trees, to be precise. Various grasses and crops were growing along irrigation ditches and the fields they watered throughout the Fertile Crescent. Small farms dotted the landscape.

I later learned that we were near al-Hillah, home to the ancient ruins at Babylon. Months later and not far from this same location I would experience the first violence directed toward me during my tour in Iraq. I was riding in the rear of a Humvee and looking out the small bulletproof window as we passed a roadside market. I was looking at three teenage boys when one whipped a stone right at my face. Of course, it bounced off the window and fell to the ground. I looked at the lad who had thrown the rock in disbelief and instantly responded by lifting up my Muslim prayer beads. I always had them with me when I traveled and began mouthing the words of a prayer in Arabic. I saw the anger in the teenager's eyes when he threw the stone; he saw the prayer on my lips as I responded.

The jaunt through the desert to Baghdad was something that I would not have wanted to miss for the life of me. It was an incredible journey, but it was also a trip I would never want to take again. Once was enough.

✠

Colonel Mike Scotto came to Baghdad and joined the Coalition Provisional Authority months after we had initially arrived at the palace. By the time he was assigned to the CPA, most of us were no longer living in the palace but had been relocated. The only people who had beds in the palace were the new arrivals whose names had been placed on a waiting list for a hooch. The hallways and vestibules of the palace had been transformed into bedrooms. Hundreds of new arrivals were herded into these spaces as their names slowly rose to the top of the housing list. Mike was one of these individuals.

I met him six days after he had arrived, when he was standing outside my office looking through the books that we made available in our "lending library." When he saw that I was a chaplain and a colonel, he began his tirade. He told me how shameful it was that he, a colonel, had to live in such deplorable conditions. He questioned the competence of those who were in charge. He went on and on, venting his frustrations with me. I am thankful and pleasantly surprised at myself in that I listened patiently. I remember thinking, "Buddy, you haven't got a clue. You've been here six days; we lived here without air conditioning throughout the entire summer. We ate MREs, and six hundred of us shared one bathroom unit with a four-stall shower and a forty-gallon hot water heater! You haven't begun to pay the dues required to comment on any of this. Why don't you get a big bowl and a straw, suck it up, and drive on?" If there's one thing I hate more than a whiney lieutenant colonel, it's a whiney colonel. Thankfully, I bit my tongue and listened patiently. I feigned empathy, but didn't have one iota of interest in listening to this "Johnny-come-lately."

Iraq is dotted with historic sights. One can visit the grave of the prophet Ezekiel. That too is located south of Baghdad, not far from al-Hillah. There are also the ancient ruins north and west of Baghdad at Hatra. Hatra was a city that was founded during the Seleucid Empire some time in the third century BCE. Seleucus ruled over a vast area that had been conquered by Alexander the Great. Hatra was also a religious and trading center during the Parthian Empire. It flourished during the first and second centuries BCE.

The Iraq Museum in Baghdad had been vandalized and robbed immediately following the invasion. Luckily enough, the staff of the museum was able to hide many of the collections. It was also fortunate that much of the statuary in the museum was too heavy to be carted off by thieves. Toward the end of my year in Baghdad, I was permitted to accompany a team of individuals on a tour of the museum. It was spellbinding. One gallery in the museum is the Hatra wing. Dozens of statues lined the walls of the Hatra wing along with stone carvings from prominent buildings. One stone mantel from a temple in Hatra portrayed a religious procession making its way to worship a pagan deity. Carved intricately into the stone were dancers and musicians playing lutes, flutes, and drums.

Iraq is itself a museum. The dry desert air has preserved the ruins at Hatra and other historic sights. Unfortunately, I never had the opportunity to visit Hatra and was never creative enough to dream up some "mission-essential task" that would require me to go there. The museum, however, did give me a taste of the ancient city.

There was one other ancient sight I wanted to visit during my year in Baghdad. It was Petra in Jordan. Petra is an amazing city carved into the stone face of towering rock walls. It has been made famous by one of the Indiana Jones films. Toward the midway point of my tour in Baghdad I mentioned to my friend Georges Sada (more about him later) that I would love to visit Petra. He was a bit surprised to learn that I had never been to Jordan to see the religious and historic sights. Georges turned to one of his companions and said, "We'll have to be sure he [meaning me] gets to Jordan. He can travel with me on one of my trips there, and I'll make arrangements for us to stay with the royal family." I couldn't believe my ears! Georges had spoken so matter-of-factly about staying with the Jordanian royal family. I savored the thought of this adventure in my mind for months, but the optempo (operations tempo) never afforded me the luxury of taking Georges up on his offer.

Colonel Mike Scotto and I ended up working together quite closely as staff officers, and we developed a wonderful relationship. I thoroughly enjoyed his sense of humor and outgoing nature. It became evident to me that I'd caught him at a bad moment when we first met. He had two significant duties during his tour in Iraq. One was as the coordinator for the convention center located directly across the street from the Al-Rasheed Hotel. The other was as the liaison for CMATT (Coalition Military Assistance Training Team) in Jordan. Mike got to visit Petra during the weeks he was stationed in Amman and told me all about it when he returned. It was hard not to be envious of his good fortune.

✣

Following a map of Iraq from south to north, one comes across the Garden of Eden, Ur of the Chaldees, Babylon and Ezekiel's tomb, Hatra. Nineveh is the northernmost. Ah, Nineveh, the ancient Assyrian city and the place where God sent Jonah to call the people to repentance. Today Nineveh is known as Mosul. I did get to visit Mosul on one occasion.

I was returning from my R&R in the United States and had to wait in Kuwait for a flight to Baghdad. Traveling by mil air (military air) is not driven by time schedules and is not a particularly pleasant way to travel, especially when flying in a C-130 cargo plane. In the first place, C-130s do not have insulation from the sound of the engines. One wears earplugs that are distributed by the crew during boarding. Secondly, the seats are long benches constructed of tubular aluminum, with nylon webbing serving as the back and bottom of the seats. It only takes me three minutes until the tube serving as the front of the seat cuts off my circulation and everything below my waist is numb. Four rows of long nylon seats run half the length of the cargo bay. Two are in the middle of the plane and face the two along the walls. Less than two feet of space separate the rows of seats. One sits down and then places his or her knees in between the knees of the person sitting directly across. If you are lucky, nothing stored behind the nylon back support is poking you in the ribs. The remainder of the cargo bay is crammed with palletized equipment being delivered to Iraq. Oh, and one more thing. The heating system in C-130s doesn't generally keep one warm. It is important to wear cold-weather gear and insulated boots for the flight.

We were fortunate, however, in that our flight did take off just about on schedule. We flew to Baghdad but for some reason did not land. It was customary for planes landing in Baghdad to have rockets launched at them with great regularity. Air Force planes carry "chaff" that is jettisoned when rockets are fired at them. The chaff is bits of metal confetti that throws off the guidance system of the rockets that have been fired and directs them away from the plane. C130 pilots have a great knack for "diving" into BIAP (Baghdad International Airport) so as to give terrorists less time to lock onto their aircraft. For whatever reason, our flight to Baghdad could not land. I suspect that the issue was related to either weather or security. Since military aircraft don't have passenger windows, I was unable to look outside to discern if our failure to land was related to bad weather or not.

DHL had an office in Saddam's former presidential palace in Baghdad. Daily DHL flights came into BIAP from Jordan. One day a terrorist rocket hit one of the jet engines on the DHL plane. The pilot managed to land the plane safely and thankfully no one was injured. It was, however, the end of DHL service in Baghdad.

The day following our aborted flight to Baghdad, we were again loaded onto a plane headed toward BIAP. The flight would not take us directly to Baghdad. We would first land in Mosul, pick up and unload passengers and equipment, and then fly on to BIAP before the crew returned to Kuwait. We landed in Mosul, quickly loaded and unloaded the plane, and were off again. My tour of Nineveh was restricted to the runway and cargo area of the base there! The plane then headed to Baghdad. For the second day in a row, however, we did not land in Baghdad. We overflew the airport and returned to Kuwait City. I had just spent two days sitting in a military air terminal and a total of seven hours in complete misery flying mil air without ever arriving at my destination. Then again, I didn't get shot down in a plane over Baghdad!

The Iraq Museum in Baghdad also had an Assyrian wing that had not been damaged by looters and vandals. Huge stone friezes weighing tens of tons depicted life in the Assyrian Empire almost four thousand years earlier. Massive Assyrian bulls carved from stone with human heads stood "guard" in the gallery. This wing of the museum was awesome and unscathed. I finally got to tour Nineveh by visiting the museum in Baghdad.

Colonel Mike Scotto reached his MRD (mandatory retirement date) while we were in Baghdad. Once a soldier reaches his or her MRD, that individual may no longer remain in the Army. Mike was interested in staying in Baghdad and was assured that an MRD extension would be granted. Unfortunately, he was misinformed! He was ordered to leave Iraq and return to CRC (CONUS [continental United States] replacement center) for out-processing. There was just one wee bit of a problem: his military ID had expired, and he could not travel on military aircraft without a valid ID card. I am not certain how this glitch was resolved, but Mike did manage to return to CONUS.

A month or so before his departure, COL Scotto came storming into our staff meeting somewhat spun up. There were some new folks at the palace who had just arrived and were bellyaching about the quality of life at the Coalition Provisional Authority. They were senior officers who were brand new and were already convinced that they knew better than everyone else did how to run the place. Mike Scotto was not amused and suggested, in not so many words, that they "get a big bowl and a straw, suck it up, and drive on!"

Chapter 5

The Reverend Canon Andrew White

Located across the street from the palace in Baghdad and about a block away is what American soldiers refer to as the "*hajji* mart." The term is not intended to give offense or used derogatorily, but it is certainly insensitive to Muslim faith and practice. The *hajj* is one of the five pillars of the Muslim religion and is required of all Muslims once in their lives if possible; it is the pilgrimage to Mecca. A *hajji* is one who has successfully completed that pilgrimage, and the title *hajji* is given to one as a term of respect.

U.S. military personnel call all Arab street vendor shops *hajji* marts. It is there that one can buy all sorts of souvenirs and gifts. Everything is available, from Arab clothing to cigarette lighters to post cards. The most popular items for U.S. military personnel are the black-market DVDs at five for twenty dollars. These DVDs are the very latest movies being released in the United States. Of course, one has to be prepared to watch a movie in which the audience is also visible. From time to time, one will see a silhouetted figure stand up, walk across the front of the theater to go to the bathroom or get popcorn, and then return to his or her seat. One must also be prepared to look at the movie from an angle when the camera filming it shifts or is bumped by the operator.

I recall reading about a movie online that was to be released in the United States in two weeks' time entitled *The Girl Next Door*. It was available at the *hajji* mart that very afternoon in Baghdad down the street from the palace. How in the world did someone pirate a copy of this movie two weeks prior to its release? The thought struck me more than once . . . so, here we are bringing law and order to Iraq while buying black market DVDs from the United States! My favorite of all the souvenirs was a particular cigarette lighter. When the top was opened, a little bomber on the cover lit up and a series of lights came on in sequence dropping from the top of the lighter to the bottom. At the bottom of the lighter, other lights made it appear as if the bombs had exploded. The English inscription on the lighter read, "Peace anxiety we!" I believe that the message on the lighter was intended to mean, "We are anxious for peace!" But who knows? I purchased a number of these lighters and sent them to friends in the United States as gifts.

British Major General (MG) Tim Cross approached me in the palace hallway one morning and asked if I might visit his office that afternoon. When a two-star general asks a colonel to visit him, one does not take that as an invitation: it is a command. He wanted to introduce me to the Rev. Canon Andrew White. Andrew was the former Archbishop of Canterbury's representative in Iraq and the Middle East. He had been traveling to Baghdad regularly for five years prior to the invasion. While (or as Andrew would say, "whilst") in Baghdad, he always visited St. George's Anglican Church to conduct services there. It was during my meeting with Andrew in MG Cross's office that he invited me to join him for services at the church upon his next visit. It was something that I keenly anticipated doing. I was curious to experience worship with the Arab Christian Community.

Andrew White served as a Canon at Coventry Cathedral. Coventry Cathedral is well known for its worldwide mission of peace and reconciliation. The cathedral has been prominent in its work in Northern Ireland, Africa, and other areas of world conflict. Canon Andrew White was their representative in Iraq and the Middle East.

Mesam Bulic was a *hajji*. He was one of the *pcelari* (Serbo-Croatian word for "beekeepers") living outside Eagle Base in Tuzla, Bosnia. He was a kind soul in his late seventies or early eighties who was one of a number of beekeepers with whom I met on a regular basis, and was a man to be respected and admired because of his pilgrimages. Apparently the United States was killing their bees inadvertently while spraying pesticides on the base from helicopters. I met with them to listen to their concerns and see what we might do to prevent further destruction to their bee colonies.

One day Mesam came to pick me up at the rear gate to Eagle Base in his Lada (Russian-made automobile) and take me to his home for a meeting with the other *pcelari* (beekeepers). Mesam was the most prominent figure in the group not only because he owned a car and was the wealthiest among them, but also because he was a *hajji*. Mesam had actually made the pilgrimage to Mecca twice in his lifetime.

It must be understood that most Bosnians take the prohibition against alcohol in the Qur'an as just a suggestion. Bosnians take great pride in their *slivovic*. *Slivo* is a brandy made from plums, and many Bosnian families make their own. It is almost impossible to attend a meeting, visit someone at home, or even call upon the sisters at the monastery and not be offered *slivovic*. Morning, noon, or night . . . it doesn't matter.

When my meeting with the *pcelari* ended, Mesam presented me with a gift. It was a bottle of *slivovic*. Following his second *hajj* two years earlier, he had determined never to drink alcoholic beverages again in his life. I believe that he wanted to make certain that he was in good graces with Allah when he died. He was getting rid of all the alcohol in his home and wanted me to take the *slivovic* as a gift. Of course, the possession or consumption of alcohol is a violation of general orders, so I had to respectfully decline his kind gift.

✠

A number of years ago, in April of 2002 to be exact, terrorists entered the Church of the Nativity in Bethlehem and held priests hostage at gunpoint. The individual who negotiated their release was Andrew White. I was immediately impressed with Canon White because he was a doer, not just a talker. Andrew had been traveling in and out of Iraq for five years prior to the invasion and was well acquainted with the political and religious leaders in the country. He was in Iraq to work with the senior religious leaders and integrate them into the quest for peace and stability. He visited Baghdad each month and remained for about a week.

During my first visit to St. George's Church with Andrew, it dawned on me that this congregation could not become stable and grow without weekly clergy support. I was struck by the faithfulness of those present and informed Andrew that I would like to conduct services at the church on a weekly basis. He consented, and my tenure at St. George's began. Following the service, Andrew, Georges Sada, and I went into the city and had dinner at a restaurant owned and operated by Christians. Following the meal, they delivered me back to the Green Zone.

✠

Violence in Baghdad is directed toward Christians for a number of reasons. One reason why some Christians were despised following the invasion is that they had been much more prosperous during Saddam's reign than many other Iraqis. Saddam employed Christians to work in his palaces. He knew that Christians wouldn't attempt to kill him. He could trust them to prepare his meals and work on the palace grounds. Many Christians were able to live quite well working for Saddam Hussein. Once the Coalition forces drove Saddam from power, the Christians who worked for him became the brunt of derision and ridicule. I guess that's the price one pays for "dancing with the devil."

Another reason why violence is directed at Christians during Ramadan is because Christians consume alcohol. The truth of the matter is that Christian alcohol producers could not sell enough alcohol to Christians to remain solvent. Iraqi Muslims also helped keep alcohol production profitable. As acts of contrition during Ramadan, however, those who had violated the Qur'an by consuming alcohol demonstrate their love for Allah by blowing up distilleries and killing the Christians who produced it.

✝

Whenever Andrew White visited Baghdad, he would join me in the chapel at the CPA for the Episcopal-Lutheran-Anglican service at 0730 hours. It was a treat for me to have a colleague with whom to share services. Andrew would also join us for the general Protestant service from time to time. Sunday afternoon he and I would travel into the city for the service at St. George's. The rest of Andrew's week involved meetings with Coalition and Iraqi leaders in the search for peace. I invited Andrew to use my office as a base of operations or to come in any time and relax. Some of the work that Andrew carried on during the week involved the release of hostages.

Many of the hostages who are kidnapped in Iraq are taken as a means for receiving a ransom. The way the hostage pipeline works is that some group of self-proclaimed "freedom" fighters or enterprising terrorists kidnap an individual or individuals and then sell them to some other like-minded group for a profit. As long as the kidnapped individual or individuals have not been purchased by al Qaeda, there is always the possibility that they can be bought back. Once they have been sold to al Qaeda, there is no way to secure their release, and they will surely be murdered. Andrew White is successful in securing the release of hostages about 33 percent of the time.

Thomas Hamill, a U.S. citizen working for Halliburton in Iraq, was kidnapped and held under guard in a small village in the middle of nowhere. Hamill escaped capture at the hands of some militant Iraqis. Now, here's Paul Harvey's "the rest of the story" as it was relayed to me by our security personnel: Hamill got free because a U.S. patrol rolled into the area where he was being held. The militant guarding him heard the Humvees and ran away. This allowed Thomas to break out of his "cell" and flag down the patrol. The patrol had actually been sent out because a report had been received the previous day regarding a break in the oil pipeline. The soldiers were to meet a team of workers at the location of the break to provide security during the repairs. There had been a glitch, however, and the patrol's headquarters had forwarded to them incorrect grid coordinates. They were three miles away from the right location. It was only because of a foul-up in communications that the patrol stumbled into him. He was one lucky guy! And that's Paul Harvey's "the rest of the story." I am not certain if Thomas Hamill ever learned the circumstances of his rescue.

✠

Mesam Bulic was taken to the hospital in Tuzla because of heart problems. I learned of his hospitalization and decided that I'd make a "pastoral" call to him. I took my linguist Besmir and we headed to the hospital. The hospital was a large facility with dozens of wards. We arrived at the front desk and asked for the room of Mesam. The hospital did not have a centralized listing of its patients, and we were pointed in the direction of another desk. After two or three stops, we finally came upon a nurse who knew where his room was.

I don't believe that we Americans have any appreciation at all for our wonderful country. No matter how bad things sometimes appear, our country is head and shoulders above other countries. We take for granted public education and public sanitation. We take for granted public transportation and human services. We take for granted lovely supermarkets and plenty to eat. We take for granted emergency services. We take for granted the enforcement of copyright laws so that no one else can profit from the illegal theft of our hard work. I could go on and on about all the benefits we enjoy as citizens of a free and democratic country. And we take it for granted that when we visit a hospital to see a loved one the people at the hospital actually know where to direct us. Until one visits a place like Bosnia or Haiti or Iraq, it is impossible to understand how lucky we Americans are.

We finally did manage to find Mesam Bulic. We visited with him and his family.

✠

Andrew White was in Iraq shortly before Christmas and needed to get a present for one of his sons. He didn't know what in the world he could find in Iraq that might be of interest to his child. I suggested that he accompany me to find some DVD that might be appropriate. The movie *Elf* had just come out in the theaters and was already available on DVD in Baghdad. It was the perfect gift for his son.

✠

Andrew White travels a great deal between Great Britain and Iraq. He also travels to the United States frequently, where he meets with Pentagon officials. He has been a guest of the televangelist Benny Hinn. He has also been a guest on *60 Minutes*, where he was referred to as "the Vicar of Baghdad." I invited him to come to Camp Arifjan, Kuwait, in 2006, where he made a presentation to the senior leaders of our command as part of our officer development program.

Andrew White was sitting in the airport in Chicago waiting for a plane, as he so often does, when the following occurred.

He was seated adjacent to an African American woman when a voice inside his head said to him, "Go over to her and tell her to name the child Rivka." (Rivka is the Hebrew name for Rachel.)

Andrew responded to this voice by saying to himself, "I'm British, we just don't do that sort of thing! We don't go over to people unknown to us and strike up a conversation. I'm not going anywhere. I'm staying right where I am." But the more Andrew persisted in staying put, the louder the voice in his mind became. "It was as if the voice of God was speaking to me," he explained. Finally, when he could resist it no longer, he got up from his seat walked over to the woman and said, "Excuse me, but there is something that I am supposed to say to you." With that he explained to the woman that a voice had been telling him to go to her and tell her to name the child Rivka.

The woman asked, "Who told you to say that to me?" Andrew explained what had happened, and the woman said. "My daughter is in the hospital giving birth, and she has told me that it is my responsibility to name the child, but I haven't come up with a name yet. Let's call her right now." With that the woman pulled out her cell phone and called her daughter. When her daughter answered, the woman said, "There's someone here who wants to speak to you," and with that she handed the phone to Andrew.

Andrew took it from the woman and spoke into the speaker, "Name the child Rivka." The girl at the other end of the call said, "Is this Father Andrew?" He replied incredulously, "How do you know me?" The girl responded, "I was part of Fr. Frank's congregation at the palace in Baghdad and you used to visit there and preach from time to time!"

Chapter 6

Georges Sada

The Coalition Provisional Authority secured ten thousand cellular phones in order to permit the members of the CPA, CJTF-7 (Combined Joint Task Force 7), principals in the new Iraqi government, and coalition partners to communicate with each other. These cell phones were all area code 917 numbers. This area code is undoubtedly familiar to the residents of New York City as one of the primary exchanges for mobile communications. This area code meant that individuals using these phones were not dependent upon the infrastructure of Iraq for voice communication. It also meant that individuals possessing these phones could call anywhere in the United States directly.

I always carried my cell phone with me wherever I went. Most U.S. soldiers protecting the compounds within the Green Zone did not have regular access to telephones and could not call home frequently. Many did have access to AT&T phones occasionally, but the cost for calling home was exorbitant. When I was stationed at Camp Arifjan, Kuwait, there was a trailer with banks of AT&T phones that permitted direct access to the United States. These phones were constantly shutting off in the middle of conversations, and the AT&T 550-minute calling card available through the PX was only good for 187 minutes when calling from Kuwait. Because of the experience of U.S. service members in theater, most have sworn never again to purchase products or services from AT&T. I considered it my responsibility in Iraq to make certain that soldiers and their families were doing OK. Upon entering a guarded compound, I would present my cell phone to the OIC or NCOIC (officer in charge or noncommissioned officer in charge) and tell that individual to call home and then pass it on to everyone on guard duty. There is no doubt that I helped run up the CPA phone bill that exceeded one million dollars a month. Fortunately or unfortunately, depending upon how one looks at it, the phone company providing service to the CPA was not able to break down individual cell phone usage and track the call made by any one phone.

The dining facility in the palace in Baghdad was as ornate as the rest of the rooms in the palace. During the early months at the palace a huge round table capable of seating ninety people took up most of the space. Saddam had used this table for formal dinners with the Baathist leadership. The area inside the horseshoe-shaped table permitted other smaller tables to be set up, and the area outside the horseshoe also permitted tables to be set up. Over time, however, the banquet table was dismantled and moved into storage because it took up far too much space. Every bit of room within the dining facility was required for seating during meals.

The cooks and personnel responsible for providing meals were all from Pakistan. They were a friendly group who loved their curry and had been subcontracted to operate the kitchen and dining room. It took a little while before they were instructed to tone down the use of curry in preparing our meals. In the dining room, serving lines had been set up, along with salad bars and dessert carousels. The dessert carousels were glass cases in which the desserts kept moving in a circular rotation until the door was opened. The desserts always looked great but never really lived up to the way they appeared. For some unknown reason, the Pakistanis just couldn't make a decent dessert to save their lives.

One evening during dinner, I spied one of the kitchen workers filling up the carousel with pieces of pie and cake. They looked scrumptious, so I got up from my table walked over to the fellow and asked, "Are the desserts any good tonight?" He looked me straight in the eyes and said with a straight face, "Maybe!" I still chuckle about it every time I remember him. His response made me take an instant liking to him that was reciprocated. Whenever he was manning the hot chocolate at the evening ice cream bar, I got an extra squirt on my ice cream.

The dining room was a great place for meeting new people. Each meal gave one the opportunity to sit with someone new and discuss the CPA efforts to reestablish the Iraqi government. One morning I ended up sitting opposite from Craig Costello, who had just arrived the evening before. He had been a Special Forces officer during his years of service in the Army and was in Baghdad to help set up the new Iraqi Department of Defense. Craig explained a little bit about his work and then asked me what my job was at the palace. I explained to him that I was the senior chaplain for the CPA. With that, he asked, "Chaplains know a lot of people. Do you know anyone who might be a possible candidate to serve in one of the top three positions in the Department of Defense for the new Iraqi government?" I did, in fact, have someone in mind and shared that name with him.

St. George's Anglican Church, Baghdad, was situated one mile north of the Green Zone on the same street as the presidential palace. It had been constructed shortly following World War I for British military and civilians working in Iraq. The church had been abandoned when the British left Iraq prior to the first Gulf War. It was evident that it had been vandalized, but for the most part it was intact. It had no lighting and no air conditioning and no church furnishings. Most of the stained glass windows were damaged, but the building would have been much worse had it not been for the fact that it was protected by the Iraqi government as a Department of State holding. It needed a complete renovation. The interior walls needed to be sandblasted, furniture needed to be purchased, and the electrical system needed to be replaced.

It did not take the CPA too long to realize that the ten thousand cell phones that had been purchased for the CPA were going fast. As a matter of fact, they were going far too fast. What had become of them all? It was decided to restrict their distribution and determine who had phones. Moreover, where possible, cell phones would be confiscated and returned to the CPA to be used later by more deserving individuals.

Life at the CPA had few amenities. The personnel assigned there did little except work and sleep. The one and only diversion was that an enterprising Iraqi who owned a pizza restaurant just outside the Green Zone was more than willing to deliver pizzas to the palace. His advertisements were taped to the walls of the palace just outside the dining facility. I noticed that he had two phone numbers for placing orders. They were both 917 area codes! These were phones that had been intended for use by the CPA. Individuals working with the various Iraqi ministries didn't have cell phones, but the pizza delivery guy did. It was also determined upon careful consideration that he would be permitted to keep the phones. It was more important to have pizza delivery to the palace than it was to collect these phones and use them for the business of the CPA. You gotta love it!

The Rev. Canon Andrew White of Coventry Cathedral introduced me to Georges Sada one afternoon during a visit to my office. Georges is small in stature, but a dynamic individual and an Assyrian Christian whose first language is Aramaic. He was a faithful Christian who headed up the Iraqi Ecumenical Council. Georges had been called back into the military prior to Operation

Desert Storm and served as the Iraqi Air Vice Marshal (equivalent to a U.S. two-star general). He had been credited with saving the lives of Coalition pilots shot down during the air campaign. When Saddam ordered them all executed, it was Georges who hid them bureaucratically so that they could not be located and executed. Georges is a courageous man of uncommon valor. It is amazing to me that he survived Saddam Hussein's regime. Georges was to become a frequent and welcome visitor to my office in the palace during my year in Baghdad. He did a great deal of good anonymously. He would never have let it be known, for example, that he, out of his own pocket, paid for the restoration work at St. George's Anglican Church. He had the building sandblasted and the electrical infrastructure reinstalled. He placed lights and ceiling fans in the church. He took a run-down, dilapidated structure and made it new again.

Georges came into my office on 14 July with ice cream for all of us. It had been so hot and miserable that it was a welcome relief to have something cold. When we were finished with the ice cream, Georges asked if he might have a private conversation with me because there was something that he needed to share. I cleared out the office so that we could chat. For forty-five minutes Georges explained to me what became of the WMD (weapons of mass destruction). He stated that they had been flown out of Iraq in the guise of relief supplies for a natural disaster. He explained to me who had flown them out of Iraq and in what type of planes. He described the types of markings on the canisters and that fifty-four or fifty-six cargo plane sorties were required to remove the WMD from Iraq. He later introduced me to one of the pilots who had flown one of the planes. He also stated that everything had been taken to Syria and given to a representative of the Syrian government. After forty-five minutes, I cut Georges off and told him that it was indeed important information, but that I wasn't the one who to whom he should be speaking. I escorted him to our intel (intelligence) people on the second floor of the palace and introduced him to them. From that moment on, Georges had unbridled access to the palace. He was welcome to visit anytime and was given an access badge that permitted him to travel in the palace unescorted.

The question I asked of Katja Bullock (Chapter 1) for President Bush was whether or not he was aware that the WMD for which the administration had been searching had been flown to Syria. I explained to her that I received this information from the former Air Vice Marshall of the Iraqi Air Force and that I had made certain that this information was passed on to our intelligence people months earlier.

Between my tour to Iraq in 2003–2004 and my tour to Kuwait in 2006–2007, I received a phone call from a gentleman who stated that he was from a new government intel oversight panel that was interested in the information Georges Sada had passed on to me. He was interested because that information may have been dismissed as either inaccurate or as coming from an unreliable source. Or, the information may have been forwarded and then not processed properly. In either case, the information had not been disseminated. Did I believe Georges? Did Georges believe that the information he received was true even if it may have been false? I answered this gentleman's questions to the best of my ability and then informed him that I would be happy to let him know the date on which I received the information from Georges. I explained that I was traveling in my car but had kept a journal during my time in Iraq and could look up the date of our conversation and inform him. I never heard back from my caller. Georges Sada published a book entitled *Saddam's Secrets*, in which he spells out the information he passed on to me in July of 2003 and some other inside information about Saddam's regime. It is a fascinating look at Baathist Iraq.

Georges Sada was the person whose name I passed on to the fellow sitting across from me at breakfast and who had come to Baghdad to get the Iraqi Ministry of Defense off the ground. I believed that Georges would be an outstanding candidate to fill one of the top three positions in the defense ministry. Ultimately Georges was flown to Washington, D.C., and met with a number of senior Pentagon officials, but the United States did not want him to fill one of the senior positions in the new Iraqi Department of Defense. They wanted Georges for more important duties. Georges was to become the primary advisor to Prime Minister Lyad Allawi in the interim Iraqi government following the departure of Ambassador Bremer and the Coalition Provisional Authority.

The Rev. Canon Andrew White, the keynote speaker at a conference of Episcopal chaplains toward the end of 2004, relayed to those present the story about Georges Sada and his appointment as chief advisor to Iyad Allawi. He then commented that I had been the individual who had picked the person who was now making the important decisions in the interim Iraqi government and the future of that country. It never ceases to amaze me how some of the seemingly insignificant encounters in our lives have the greatest consequence. I was only sitting at breakfast having a chat with someone who had just arrived at the CPA.

✢

The evening before I left Iraq at the end of my tour, Andrew White and Tom Kingston (Andrew's assistant) gathered a number of my friends, including Georges Sada, and took me out to dinner at a restaurant that had just opened in the Green Zone. It was a most unforgettable meal, and not simply because of the thoughtfulness of my friends. It was unforgettable because of the meal itself. Knowing that I like lamb, Georges had suggested that the restaurant prepare an entire lamb on a spit and bring it to our table on a huge tray surrounded by mounds of rice. All of us shared from the common tray. When one of us wanted more food, someone grabbed a handful of rice or ripped off a piece of lamb and put it on our individual plates. It was a meal in true Arab fashion. After a time, I lost my appetite, not only because I was stuffed, but also because the restaurant in which we were eating was a tent. Hundreds of flies had found their way to our table and were also feasting on the lamb along with us.

✢

Following my return to the United States, I was thinking of my good friend Georges. I did not know that he was serving as the primary advisor to Allawi and called him on his cell phone. After all, it was just a local cell phone-to-cell phone call, since he had a 917 area code. I didn't actually know if he had retained the same phone number, and I was a bit surprised when someone else answered the phone. I was certain that the phone was no longer Georges'. I told the person who answered that I was Abuna or Abouna (the Arab word for father . . . it was what the people at St. George's Anglican Church called me) Frank and was calling for Georges. He informed me that Georges was in a private meeting with the Prime Minister. "Just a moment," he said, and I heard a knock on the door. Then I heard a muffled voice say, "Abuna Frank is on the phone for you." I then heard Georges say, "You'll have to excuse me, Prime Minister, while I take this call."

✢

Was the information Georges received regarding the weapons of mass destruction correct? Were the WMD flown to Syria by pilots from the Iraqi Air Force well known to Georges Sada? If for a moment we accept the premise that WMD were flown to Syria, as reported to me and stated in *Saddam's Secrets*, then why has the Bush Administration kept silent about this? Wouldn't this be vindication for the invasion of Iraq? Or, is it possible that if such a thing could be proven, it would mean that a confrontation with Syria is inevitable?

Three possible scenarios regarding the issue of WMD are plausible to me. First, Georges Sada was given accurate information regarding the flights into Syria, but acting on that information would cause an expansion of the war into Syria, which the United States is not prepared to initiate militarily or diplomatically. Second, the information that he was given regarding the flight of WMD into Syria is inaccurate, or he is not considered a reliable source. Third, the information he presented regarding WMD cannot be independently verified and cannot, therefore, be claimed by the Bush administration as a justification for the invasion of Iraq.

Whatever the case, Georges Sada is convinced that Iraq possessed weapons of mass destruction and that they were transported by pilots he trained and trusted to Syria shortly before the invasion began.

Chapter 7

Maher Dahkil

The Mandeans (also known as Sabaeans) are a religious sect of Iraq slightly older than Christianity. The Mandeans are the direct descendent of the disciples of John the Baptist. Their religious rituals involve baptism (immersion in water) on those occasions that are the significant rites of passage in life. Mandeans, unlike Christians who are baptized only once, will be baptized numerous times during their lives.

One of the Mandean baptisms occurs at the time of marriage. A Mandean priest joins the bride and groom, who are both dressed in white baptismal gowns, in matrimony. He separately baptizes them, has them drink from the "holy water" of the Tigris River, and then joins them together as husband and wife. I once questioned a Mandean about the wedding ritual, especially in regard to drinking water from the Tigris River. The Tigris River is incredibly polluted by the time it winds it way through Baghdad. Every kind of sewage imaginable, including dead carcasses, finds its way into the water of the Tigris before faithful Sabaeans drink from it as part of their nuptials. I was informed that Mandeans are convinced that they cannot be harmed when drinking from the Tigris as an act of their faith. It was also made clear to me that the most important thing to do when drinking from the Tigris River is to hold the cup of water in one hand and pinch one's nostrils with the other.

The fact that Mandeans are baptized on many occasions throughout the course of their lives has led me to consider the possibility that John the Baptist may have baptized individuals on more than one occasion. It is possible that the present Mandean baptismal rituals have grown out of the ministry of John the Baptist and been handed down within the Sabaean community directly from him. If this is so, it is possible that John immersed Jesus more than once. The Christian scriptures recount one occasion on which John baptized Jesus in the Jordan River. The Christian scriptures are not, however, a detailed account of every aspect of the entire life of Jesus. Could it be that John baptized his cousin Jesus numerous times? Is it possible that only one of Jesus' baptisms was reported in the gospel narrative?

U.S. Army personnel are required to annually receive briefings on a number of topics. These briefings are repeated during the mobilization process for reserve forces and cover such topics as the Law of Land Warfare. Officers from the Staff Judge Advocate Corps (JAGs) present these briefings, and all soldiers are required to attend them. It is also required that all personnel attending these briefings print and sign their names on a roster to prove they have received the training. Soldiers who have not been present at the required briefings may not be deployed into the theater of combat operations. Many Reserve and Guard units deploying into the theater brief their soldiers prior to their arrival at the mobilization station. What these units discover is that all of the training conducted before arriving at the MOB site will have to be conducted again by the cadre at the mobilization station. In other words, deploying soldiers will be required to attend all briefings after arriving at the mobilization station even if they attended those briefings just a few days earlier at their unit's home station. The briefing on the Law of Land Warfare stresses the humane treatment of enemy prisoners of war. U.S. military personnel are instructed that once an enemy soldier has been disarmed, he or she is no longer a combatant. Furthermore, it is made perfectly clear that the proper care of wounded enemy prisoners of war is a requirement for U.S. forces.

The inhumane treatment of the prisoners at Abu Ghraib was not just an embarrassment for the Bush administration, Secretary of Defense Donald Rumsfeld, and the senior ranking military officers on the ground. It was a repudiation of everything every American soldier is taught and has drilled into him or her regularly. It was an inhumane action, the consequences of which likely led to more combat causalities. The public outrage of the Iraqi people in response to the actions at Abu Ghraib did not get directed toward those who perpetrated the acts. Their outrage spilled over onto other U.S. military personnel, who became the brunt of IEDs and mortar and rocket attacks. The reason why U.S. military personnel are trained to treat enemy prisoners of war humanely is not merely because it is the right thing to do or because a failure to do so is bad press for America. U.S. military personnel are trained to treat captives humanely because they are the ones who will eventually pay the price for a failure to do so. It is a matter of self-preservation. Soldiers are not fond of those who bring fire down on their position!

The 28th CSH (combat support hospital) was located in the Green Zone not far from the former presidential palace. The doctors, nurses, and staff of the 28th CSH not only were responsible for treating coalition military and civilian personnel but also treated Iraqi nationals who were brought to them following suicide bombings and other catastrophic events. The hospital in the Green Zone was a sophisticated operation with all the services one would expect in any hospital in the United States. There was even an information desk at the front entrance. Everything that we Americans associate with good medical care was present at this Army hospital. The patient wards were located on the second floor of the facility. Patients in recovery or awaiting transport out of theater were monitored there. One ward, however, was different from the rest. A guard was stationed there for the safety of all in the hospital. This was the ward in which enemy combatants were being treated. They may have been former Iraqi Republican Guard soldiers or foreign terrorists who had been wounded by U.S. forces during a firefight. One fellow was a suicide bomber who had been only partially successful. He had managed to detonate the device strapped to him and had also managed to blind and maim himself, but he had survived the explosion. He was now being given the high quality of medical care that one expects will be provided to U.S. military personnel admitted to the hospital.

The first Sunday afternoon that I visited St. George's Anglican Church in Baghdad to lead worship was an unforgettable experience. Following the service, I was standing outside the church building, speaking to Maher Dahkil. Maher worked as a translator for the U.S. military. The U.S. military hires both linguists and translators for work with our forces when deployed internationally. Linguists are individuals who are fluent in English and can help military personnel converse with the local nationals. Translators are those who are not only fluent in English but can also read and write English and thus translate documents from or into English. Maher worked within the Green Zone as a translator at the 28th CSH. He assisted the hospital staff in communicating with Iraqis who were brought in for treatment. He also visited with Iraqi nationals who had been admitted to the hospital.

One of the things I have discovered about individuals who are converts to anything is that they are more ardent in their beliefs than those who have grown up with the things in which they believe. Maher Dahkil was no exception. Maher was a convert to Christianity from Mandeanism. He possessed a burning desire to share his newfound beliefs with everyone with whom he came into contact. He explained to me that he visited the suicide bomber and other Muslim terrorists in the hospital wards and always shared his faith with them. He encouraged them to embrace Christianity and renounce their life of terrorism.

I was the only non–Arabic speaker at St. George's when I went there to conduct services. Maher served as my linguist during worship. He would also pick me up in the Green Zone and escort me to the church in his 1983 beat-up white Toyota sedan (I'll come back to his car in a bit). As I said, I was speaking with Maher following my first Sunday conducting services at St. George's. It is customary following worship that groups of people will chat with each other to catch up on one another's activities. I spied a small group of people chatting rather loudly about some topic, turned to Maher and inquired, "Maher what are they talking about?" He responded, "I haven't got a clue. They're speaking Aramaic."

Aramaic was the language of Jesus. I was taught in seminary that it was a dead language and lost forever to the world. But here in Baghdad I had just worshipped with people who still speak the language of Jesus. I felt as if I had been transported back into the Bible. I was living in the land of the Garden of Eden with people who spoke Aramaic. What was even more incredible is that the person who was my translator had not that long ago been a follower of John the Baptist. This was the adventure of a lifetime!

✠

My Sundays in Baghdad followed a daily pattern. I conducted an Episcopal-Lutheran-Anglican service at 0730 hours in the chapel at the palace. I then led a general Protestant service at 1000 hours at the palace. On Sunday afternoons, Maher arrived at the palace to pick me up and secret me out of the Green Zone to St. George's Anglican Church. I conducted a 1600 hours service there and then went to Maher's home for dinner following the worship. Since the service at St. George's was always two hours long and dinner followed, I didn't generally return to the Green Zone until about 2100 hours. Actually, my Sunday routine began at noon on Saturday. For it was at about noon on Saturday that the struggle within me started regarding whether or not I would be putting my life on the line by going to St. George's the following day. Traveling out of the Green Zone always carried with it the possibility for injury or death. And worshipping with a Christian Community in Iraq was also cause for concern. Churches were being bombed and Christians murdered at church on Sunday by terrorists. The decision to go to Church in Iraq is not simply a matter of what one is to wear or a question of whether or not one feels likes going. It is a life-and-death decision that places one in a very precarious position. I would be traveling out of the Green Zone in Maher's old Toyota.

We in the United States take for granted that the automobiles we see on the road are safe to be driven. Cars that are imported by individuals into the

U.S. must meet government safety regulations. If one were to buy a car in Europe and then have it shipped to the United States, many upgrades would need to be made before it can be registered to be operated. This is not the case in Iraq. Not only was Maher's car old, it was a wreck! The windshield had a number of cracks running lengthwise. The doors didn't all open, and the lights didn't work well at night. Lord knows what else was the matter with the car. It was certainly not a vehicle that one could trust on a long journey.

Maher would appear across the street from the palace in his car. I would hop in wearing civilian clothes, and he would drive me out one of the Green Zone gates to the church. Chaplains do not carry weapons, so I had no means of defending myself against armed attack. Moreover, by leaving the Green Zone with Maher unescorted by security or military personnel I was violating all force protection protocols. The thing I worried about the most in contemplating my weekly pilgrimage to St. George's was not being killed. It was the possibility of being wounded or kidnapped and held for ransom. Had that happened, I would have been a world of trouble because I knowingly violated U.S. policy! After I arrived at St. George's and greeted members of the congregation, the turmoil I experienced about going to church vanished. I was with a wonderful community of Christians who were dedicated to their faith and their Lord. Once I was caught up in the worship, all fears vanished, and I was pleased that I'd determined to lead worship for one more week. I do remember one Sunday, however, when Maher called to inform me that he would be unable to travel into the Green Zone. The gates had been locked down for security purposes in response to a recent attack. When I learned that I wouldn't be traveling to church that day, I must admit that I was relieved.

One Sunday following church, as I ate dinner with Maher, his wife, and his daughter and son, explosions erupted in the neighborhood around Maher's house. We all went up on his roof to see what was going on and saw a number of fires in homes on streets nearby. Later I was to learn that a terrorist had intended to attack the Green Zone with a dozen rockets. He was rather inept at his trade, and all the rockets landed in Maher's neighborhood. What immediately dawned on me is that our security personnel at the entrances to the Green Zone would be on heightened alert. What if Maher's old Toyota had bad brakes? What if we could not stop when ordered to by the Iraqi and American soldiers? I'd end up getting killed by my own folks! As it turned out, Maher's car did halt at the checkpoint, and I was permitted to walk a mile and a half back to the palace.

Two events stand out in my mind during the eight months I led worship at St. George's Anglican Church, Baghdad. The first occurred at Christmas time, and the second just prior to Easter. The two events were similar in nature.

I had just finished leading the service, and the women of the congregation were bringing their children forward for me to bless them. Suddenly at the entrance to the church fifteen Muslim women escorted by two Muslim men appeared. They had been across the street at a wedding reception for a Muslim couple and had seen the light on the cross of the church lit up. They left the reception and came into the church looking for blessings on the newlyweds from Jesus. I think that they wanted some sort of icon with Jesus' picture on it to take back to the reception.

The other occasion that stands out in my mind took place in much the same manner as the visit by the women from the wedding reception. This time five Muslim women entered the church at the end of the service and were near the entrance looking for something. I asked Maher to inquire of them what they wanted. He reported back to me that they were members of an extended family all living together in a two-room apartment. And guess what? They were having trouble getting along with one another. They had come to the church seeking blessings from Jesus and the Virgin Mary. I asked Maher to speak with them and find out if they would like me, the Christian priest, to pray with them. In a moment he returned with the women and we formed a circle in the nave of the church, and I prayed for them in the name of Jesus Christ and asked his blessing upon them and their family.

Then something very strange and unexpected happened. One of the women for whom I had just prayed stated through Maher that she had been having back pain for years and would I pray for her for healing. I asked Maher if it would be all right for me to lay hands on her while praying. There was no way in the world that I was going to touch a Muslim woman without permission! She gave her assent, and I laid hands on her and prayed. I don't know how what I said in English translated into Arabic. I can tell you that Maher's translation was quite a bit longer than my prayer. It was evident that he knew exactly what Arab women expect to hear proclaimed in a prayer and had loosely translated what I said. Following my prayer another of the women asked that I lay hands on her and pray because of some other ailment. Again Maher translated what I had said and went on for quite some time.

Maher had been imprisoned by Saddam's security forces for preaching Jesus Christ to Muslims following his conversion to Christianity. I am not exactly certain how long he was in prison, but it was for a period of months. He was released in extraordinary fashion. The story he told me about his release appears to have jumped right out of the pages of the New Testament.

Maher was the only Christian in jail with Sunni and Shia Muslims. One of the Sunnis became very sick and was getting progressively worse. Maher challenged him to pray for healing in whatever manner he desired. He invited the others in prison with this fellow to pray for him as well. After a few days, Maher prayed for him in the name of Jesus and claimed that he would be cured only in his name. The following day the fellow was better.

Maher shared a similar story regarding a Shia prisoner. This fellow too had been sick. Maher therefore challenged him to pray in whatever manner he desired to be healed. He challenged the other prisoners to pray for this man. The fellow just got worse. Finally, Maher prayed for this person and the following day he was better.

The guards of the prison who had witnessed these two events were amazed at this "holy man." Even though Maher had committed a capital offense by preaching Christianity to Muslims, they were going to release him on their own and without any authority whatsoever to do so. That is how Maher was released from prison.

I find Arab culture fascinating. It was on my second or third visit to Maher's home for dinner following church that he informed me that I was to consider his home my home. I was also informed that I was part of his family. His home was not a grand house. It was a small place with living room, kitchen, three bedrooms upstairs, and a bathroom. The house was situated in a walled-in compound along with his in-laws' house right next door. His in-laws and cousins were all still Mandeans. I had a standing invitation to attend one of their rituals but never had the opportunity to take advantage of the invitation. We would sit in the living room of Maher's home and eat dinner with the television on in the background. Watching television was particularly important to Maher and his family because satellite television had been against the law in Saddam's Iraq. They wanted to learn what the outside world had to say. They were eager for information that hadn't been filtered by Saddam's regime. It was evident that they were not alone in this desire because satellite dishes began to appear throughout Baghdad.

Maher's wife was a devout Christian who was his partner in ministry. They visited members of the church and arranged for food, clothing, and medicine for those in need. Maher's daughter was a college student in Baghdad majoring in English. The entire family was fluent, and it was easy to carry on discussions about Iraqi religion and culture with them. Maher's son was also very active at St. George's. The music at St. George's was generally accompanied by a tape recorder. Maher's son decided that we should have live music, so Maher purchased an electronic keyboard for him and he practiced the Sunday hymns all week long. I can tell you that what he lacked in musical ability he more than made up for in volume!

✠

Maher would always say that the American forces needed to remain in Iraq for a long time. He was convinced that life had become much better since the invasion and the majority of Iraq people were glad that Saddam was gone.

I had to stop conducting services at St. George's Anglican Church shortly following Easter Sunday in 2004. It was becoming widely known that an American was leading the worship there, and my presence was increasing the likelihood of violence at the church. Many in the Muslim community also knew I was there, and it seemed prudent that I stop leading the weekly worship. Prior to departing Baghdad, I invited Maher and his family to visit me in the Green Zone for dinner. I met them at the pedestrian gate and we had a wonderful meal together at the Al-Rasheed Hotel.

Following my return to the United States after my year in Baghdad, I corresponded with Maher and received the following e-mail from him following the first election there in February of 2005. He wrote,

> Thank you for being always in feelings with us,
>
> It was a great day that many iraqis accepted the challenge, in atmosphere fill with challenge, fear, mortars, gun shootings and sucidal bombings, many iraqis had decided to go and vote whatever the consequences are.
>
> I had encouraged my congregation to pray before they decide to go for voting, i had taken my wife and my daughter (she is in her 2nd year of college), i told my daughter that for her this is the first time in her life to go to vote but it is also the first time for her father also, i am 48 and i am voting freely for the first time in my life.
>
> We were proud and happy it was a historical day in our life.
>
> maher
> baghdad

✠

When I reflect upon my time in Baghdad, I know that I was happiest with Maher, his family, and the people of St. George's Anglican Church. The first Sunday that I attended church fifty-three people attended. The last Sunday that I led worship the congregation had grown to two hundred and twenty. I know that this was due in large measure to the faithful work of Maher and his family. The Anglican Church of St. George's, Baghdad, has now grown to more than eight hundred people.

Following my note from Maher in February, he, his wife, his son, and another wonderful Christian friend, Farias, disappeared while returning from a Christian conference in Jordan. It is evident that they were robbed and murdered somewhere in the area of Fallujah. Their bodies have never been recovered.

✝

One of the privileges we enjoy as citizens of a free and prosperous nation is the right to freedom of religion. We can worship and pray as we see fit. It is a freedom that is closely guarded by many of our religious leaders. The possible erosion of our right to religious freedom is a hotly debated topic in our body politic. Whenever the topic presents itself, however, I always hearken back to something I was taught as a child in Sunday school. I learned that "the Church is built on the blood of the martyrs." And do you know? I have come to believe that this is the truth. I am convinced that the church prospers not so much when it is endowed with guaranteed freedoms from the state but when martyrs are made of the faithful. My experience at St. George's Anglican Church, Baghdad, has confirmed for me what I learned in Sunday school as a child.

The church in Baghdad is not being built upon the eight months that I led worship there. It is being built upon her martyrs who truly were my friends and my family during my year in Baghdad: Maher, his wife and son, and Farias.

Chapter 8

Beth Payne

General Order #1 establishes a commanding general's guidance for the good order and discipline of his or her troops. General Orders #1 in the theater of operations in Iraq, Afghanistan, and Kuwait share many items in common. They prohibit the possession of drugs and alcohol. They prohibit the cohabitation of individuals of the opposite sex, and disallow males from entering the living quarters of females and vice versa. General Orders #1 prohibit pornography, entering mosques without express permission, and gambling. They also prohibit the use of personal weapons or their transport to the United States if acquired as "war trophies." Military personnel who violate General Order #1 are subject to judicial punishment under the Uniform Code of Military Justice (UCMJ).

As I saw it, there were a number of flaws in General Order #1. First, it was a one-size-fits-all approach to discipline and order. For example, married couples who were deployed together were not permitted to share the same living quarters. They couldn't even visit each other's billets. I deployed with two married colonels who were not permitted to live together during their year-long deployment.

Second, the theory and practice of General Order #1 do not always coincide with the reality of life in the theater of operations. Pornography is prohibited. Pornographic material in much of the Arab world is defined as pictures of women with their arms uncovered. Military personnel were warned not to enter theater with "revealing" pictures of their spouses (i.e., it was advisable not to have pictures of them in short sleeves). The prohibition against pornography included the possession of "muscle" magazines and other magazines with pictures of women scantily clad. Of course, one could purchase these magazines at the PX without penalty. Bringing them into the country or receiving them in the mail, however, subjected one to prosecution under UCMJ.

Finally, the Army has never really invented anything that is "soldier proof," including General Order #1. Soldiers will always attempt to find a way to circumvent anything that stands in the way of something they desire.

A civil affairs team consisting of a major, two NCOs, and a specialist thought it would be a good idea to have a barbecue late one night. The location they selected was the Baghdad zoo. We all know that no cookout is complete without alcohol, so these soldiers had lots to drink while barbecuing their chicken. After they were well intoxicated, it seemed like a great idea to the specialist to share some of the barbecued chicken with the zoo's tiger. The only difficulty was that the tiger was confined behind two secure metal cages. The solution for having the tiger enjoy the party was to break into the outer cage, which was accomplished by breaking the lock. The inner cage was constructed of rebar (rebar is that which is used to reinforce concrete) spaced about an inch and a half apart. The specialist took some of the chicken on a spit and managed to get his hand in between the pieces of rebar holding the spit. Guess what? Tigers prefer hand to chicken, and this one pulled the specialist's arm all the way into the cage up to his shoulder. One can only imagine the physical damage that occurred to this specialist's arm as the skin and muscle were ripped apart. The specialist began screaming, and his barbecue buddies came to his rescue. They shot and killed the tiger with an unauthorized weapon! One of them had either brought a personal weapon into theater (which is hard to believe) or had found an Iraqi weapon and been carrying that around. Let's see now. A team of soldiers held a barbecue in an unauthorized location with alcohol, a clear violation of General Order #1. They broke into a cage at the zoo and then proceeded to kill the zoo's only tiger with an unauthorized weapon, another clear violation of General Order #1.

The following day I went to the zoo and met with the director. He introduced me to the gentleman who was responsible for the tiger. The tiger keeper had raised the tiger its entire life. He showed me the mound of earth on top of the grave he had dug and in which he had buried the animal. With tears in his eyes, he told me all about the animal he had lovingly raised. A very unchaplainlike thought ran through my mind as I heard the grief in the tiger keeper's voice: they should have shot the specialist!

Two National Guard soldiers from Florida made an appointment to come to my office and speak with me. They had been in Iraq for almost three months and had met two lovely Iraqi women while on patrol in the city. The relationships between these two soldiers and the two women had developed to the point where they wanted to get married. The reason that they had come to speak with me is because, according to Iraqi law, they were required to convert to Islam. These soldiers were Christians.

I must point out that it is not possible for U.S. military personnel deployed to Iraq to be married by U.S. military chaplains. Marriages require marriage licenses issued by a state. It is the state that appoints individuals who are approved to conduct marriage rites. U.S. military chaplains are not authorized by other countries to conduct marriages. According to Iraqi law, any non-Muslim man marrying a Muslim woman must convert to Islam. The converse is not true, however. A non-Muslim woman marrying a Muslim man may retain her religion. The two soldiers wanted to discuss the implications of converting to the Muslim faith. No, they didn't really believe in Islam. They were just going to pretend to convert. When they returned to the United States, they'd continue to be Christians and raise their children in the church.

I attempted to share with these two soldiers a number of issues for them to consider before proceeding. Muslims who abandon the faith are apostates. Apostasy in some Arab countries is punishable by death. Let us say, for example, that they did decide to get married to the Muslim women and convert. And let us further suppose that they had children, but that their marriages ended in divorce. If their former spouses returned to the Middle East or Southwest Asia with the children, these men would not be able to follow. They would never be given their children in an Arab court proceeding. Moreover, they might very well be tried as apostates and sentenced to death.

Beth Payne served as the United States Consul in Baghdad. She was a young, extremely knowledgeable woman who had served in embassies of the United States in the Arab world. She was very familiar with Arab culture and religion. She was also very astute concerning the motivation of Arab women who want to marry U.S. citizens. According to Beth, the great majority of these women are only doing so to become U.S. citizens themselves. They do not in most cases love the people they are marrying. There are many cases in which the "couple" to be married cannot even communicate with each other. The Arab cannot speak English and the American doesn't know a word of Arabic.

The two American soldiers from the Florida National Guard who wanted to marry the Iraqi women were thirty-eight and forty years of age. The two Iraqi women were twenty-five years old. The women were both doctors. The soldiers were lower-ranking individuals. It certainly gave one pause for consideration.

Shortly following my arrival in Trinidad in support of the Marines of the 8th ESB (Engineer Support Battalion) in 1996, the company commander asked to speak to me. "Sir," he said, "I have a young Marine who wants to talk to you."

The 8th ESB had only been in Trinidad about two weeks, and I was curious what might have occurred in that short a period of time that made it necessary for a Marine to speak with the chaplain.

"Well, sir, the Marine wants to get married and he needs your permission to do so." I guess it was the policy in the Marine Corps for Marines to have the permission from a chaplain to get married.

I asked, "Captain, who does he want to marry?"

I figured it was some sweetheart back home or a girlfriend at Camp Lejeune. "Sir, he just met a prostitute a week ago here in Trinidad and he's in love and wants to get married."

"Captain," I said, "I'm happy to speak to this young Marine, but you can inform him that I am not giving him permission to get married. He may hate me for the rest of his life, but I am not giving him permission to marry a prostitute to take back home and introduce to mom and the family." The Marine never did come and speak with me.

General Order #2 was a policy developed by the CJTF-7 (Combined Joint Task Force 7) JAG office. It was a document that prevented the marriage of U.S. military personnel and Iraqi nationals. I suspect that the development of General Order #2 was initiated by LTG Ricardo Sanchez, CJTF-7 Commanding General. I reviewed it in draft form when it was presented to me by the CJTF-7 JAG. The military "staffs" policies before publishing them. "Staffing" entails circulation of proposed policies to staff principals for input and concurrence or nonconcurrence. Although I was not on the CJTF-7 staff, this was being forwarded to me as a courtesy. I was also asked for input. It was not my position to concur or nonconcur. It was well known at the palace that I had met with military personnel who were interested in marrying Iraqi nationals and was planning to conduct a seminar to explore the intricacies of Arab-American marriages.

General Order #2 never survived the staffing process and was never issued as a command policy by CJTF-7. At that time, I suspected it died a natural death because it would have been politically embarrassing to let it be known that the U.S. military was preventing its personnel from falling in love and getting married. It may have also been embarrassing for the U.S. to have the world discover that although the U.S. and Iraq were partners in democracy, Iraqi nationals were not good enough to marry American soldiers or to become U.S. citizens. Or, it may have been that General Order #2 was just not enforceable. What would happen in the event that a National Guard or Reserve soldier completed a tour of active duty and then returned to Iraq as a "civilian" to marry an Iraqi? Would General Order #2 apply or not? Was the individual a soldier (because of his or her reserve status) or a civilian?

✠

The two soldiers from the Florida National Guard did end up marrying the two Iraqi women, in violation of a direct order from their battalion commander. They enlisted the assistance of their NCOs to make this happen. Apparently, they went out on patrol with other members of their unit and met the brides at a prearranged location in Baghdad. The families of the women were there, along with an individual licensed by the Iraqi government to perform weddings. When the wedding started, they put down their weapons and the nuptials were performed. The service ended and they and their buddies continued with the patrol. I am not certain whether or not there was a reception but would not be surprised if that occurred as well. What I do know, from the perspective of a senior ranking officer in the U.S. Army, is that their little stunt jeopardized the lives of all involved in a non-mission-oriented event.

I do remember that following the wedding these soldiers were restricted to their base of operations until they redeployed to the U.S. They never saw their brides in Iraq following their wedding day. I am also aware that punitive action was initiated upon their return to Florida. I am not certain what their fate was, and I am not certain if their wives ever joined them in the United States.

I am not opposed to love. I am most certainly not against the marriage of American soldiers to Iraqi nationals. I do, however, concur with the battalion commander who forbade the marriage of his soldiers. I also concur with his decision to take action against them. These soldiers placed other unit members at risk by stopping in the midst of a patrol in Baghdad to get married. They put the entire patrol in danger by stopping at an unsecured location and holding a marriage ceremony. They placed their brides and their brides' families in danger of injury and death.

The reason that the trips I coordinated to the ruins at ancient Babylon ended is that our convoy was IEDed one Friday on our return to the Green Zone from al-Hillah. Following the attack upon our convoy, we could no longer justify placing U.S. personnel at risk for non-mission-essential activities. It is one thing to place oneself at risk; it is quite another thing to risk the lives of one's fellow soldiers for personal reasons.

The direct supervisors of these soldiers also demonstrated incredibly poor judgment by stopping at an unknown location in Baghdad while on patrol. Thankfully for everyone involved, no one was killed or wounded during the patrol. This is the kind of thing for which an entire chain of command from the NCOIC (noncommissioned officer in charge) all the way up to the battalion commander can be relieved from duty and prosecuted under the UCMJ.

Beth Payne and I did conduct a "marriage seminar" at the palace one evening for U.S. military and civilian personnel who were contemplating marriage to Iraqi nationals. More than a dozen individuals attended the session. There were dozens of budding romances in the palace between Iraqi day workers and soldiers or civilians attached to the Coalition Provisional Authority.

I believed that it was my responsibility as a pastor and as the senior chaplain for the CPA to do everything within my power to assist individuals in making mature, adult decisions with regard to the marriage of Iraqi nationals. I viewed the seminar as a sort of premarital counseling group session. With the assistance of Beth Payne, we discussed issues of religion, culture, and laws concerning the marriage of U.S. citizens and nationals from Arabic countries.

Beth Payne's observations were eye-opening. The U.S. Department of State does not grant entrance into the U.S. to foreign nationals just because they marry Americans. Foreign nationals must be able to demonstrate that their marriage is based upon love and not as a means of gaining U.S. citizenship for themselves or family members. Couples must demonstrate that they have a stable, long-term relationship and not a fly-by-night fling. U.S. citizens marrying foreign nationals must demonstrate that they have the financial resources to support a spouse. This is to ensure that the spouse will not become a ward of the state and a burden on the U.S. taxpayer. Moreover, Beth highlighted that the processes for attaining a visa can take as much as a year or more.

It was also made clear to the U.S. military personnel present that marriage to an Iraqi national would impact one's security clearance. It was probable that military personnel whose jobs required a security clearance would lose their clearance and therefore their military jobs.

Not long after the marriages of the two Iraqi women to the soldiers from the Florida National Guard, I received a phone call from one of the directorates within the CPA. The two women had received threats against their lives for marrying American soldiers. The individual who called me wanted to know what the CPA would do to help them. She actually wanted us to bring them into the Green Zone, find housing for them, and secure jobs for them with the

CPA or a contractor located inside the Green Zone. I in turn contacted the CJTF-7 JAG regarding the Army's legal responsibility toward the spouses of service members. I did believe that we had a moral obligation to assist them in every way possible.

It may have been that General Order #2 was intended for the good order and discipline of U.S. military personnel in Iraq. It may have been that General Order #2 was intended to prevent U.S. military personnel from compromising the safety and security of themselves and Iraqi nationals. It may have been that General Order #2 was intended to mitigate U.S. responsibility toward the spouses of U.S. military personnel living in danger outside the Green Zone. It may have been that General Order #2 was intent on preventing security degradation. Whatever the original intent, General Order #2 was never published.

I wish that I could report what actually became of the two Iraqi women who married the soldiers from the Florida National Guard. Were they murdered for marrying Americans? Were they granted a safe haven and jobs in the Green Zone? Did they ultimately find their way to the United States? Are they now living with their husbands?

Chapter 9

Chaplain (Commander) Emilio Marrero

U.S. Army

The 1st Marine Expeditionary Force (1 MEF) established their base of operations near al-Hillah, encircling the ancient ruins of Babylon. They named their base Camp Babylon. It was a good thing they that chose to do so, because looters had already stolen some ancient artifacts from the site. They had vandalized the museum and gift shop.

The ruins at Babylon are religiously and historically significant for many reasons. One reason for its importance is that Babylon was the place of the Babylonian captivity, the deportation of the Jews from Jerusalem in 586 B.C.E. Another reason why Babylon is important is that Alexander the Great died there at the zenith of his power.

Saddam Hussein took great interest in the ruins at Babylon and appointed archeologists to rebuild the walls of Babylon upon the ancient foundations. This was considered an archeological disaster by most if not all archeologists. He also had an earthen mound built on top of a portion of the ruins near the site of King Nebuchadnezzar's palace. The mound was built in order that Saddam could have a new palace erected overlooking the ruins. The Marines commandeered the palace and used it as a barracks for enlisted personnel.

Prior to the invasion of Iraq, the United Nations had managed what became known as the Oil-for-Food Programme. The purpose of the program was to permit the people of Iraq to receive necessary humanitarian aid. After serving in Iraq for a few months, all of us began to call it the "oil for palaces" program. While the people of Iraq basically had nothing, Saddam Hussein built ornate palaces all over the country. This is what became of the money he (not Iraq) received in exchange for oil. U.S. military personnel were flabbergasted at the dichotomy between Saddam's wealth and the poverty of his people.

In 1996, I spent my reserve annual training in support of the 8th ESB (Engineer Support Battalion) in Trinidad. The 8th ESB is a Marine Corps Battalion (BN) and was responsible for three construction projects on the island. I was a member of the 358th Civil Affairs Brigade (CA BDE) that served as liaison between the "Trini" government and the Marines of the 8th ESB. The 358th's area of operation was the Caribbean, and the members of our unit were continually deployed to the islands. Members of the civil affairs community jokingly referred to the 358th as BEACHCOM (beach command) because we spent all of our time in the sunny Caribbean.

I thoroughly enjoyed my seventeen days with the 8th ESB. Marines are super. They have a "can do" attitude that is infectious. In my entire association with the Marine Corps, I have never heard a Marine tell anyone that something could not be accomplished. I have never heard a Marine gripe about any assignment regardless of how difficult or idiotic it may have appeared. Actually, I have never heard a Marine complain about anything. I believe that had I to do it over again, I might have become a Navy chaplain and requested to be assigned to the Marines. The Marine Corps does, however, have its own unique way of handling things.

✢

The members of the 416th Civil Affairs Company (a subordinate unit of the 358th CA BDE) were informed at our unit drill in December of 1990 that we were not being mobilized in support of Operation Desert Storm. Later that month, on 27 December to be exact, I received a phone call from the 416th's unit administrator informing me that I was being mobilized in support of Desert Storm. I remember saying to him that I hadn't thought our unit would be mobilized in light of what we had been told at the December drill. He responded, "The unit hasn't mobilized, you have!" I was to be cross-leveled (i.e., transferred) to another unit along with ten other members of our command.

A good friend of mine from the unit and our JAG was also mobilized. I didn't see Roger Ullman very much following our deployment to Saudi Arabia. I was assigned to the 401st Civil Affairs Company and worked at the port of Damam while Roger was assigned to work with the Marines based at al-Jubail. I am convinced that Roger was thrilled with his assignment because he had enlisted in the Marine Corps years earlier and served in the Marines prior to becoming a JAG officer in the Army. Serving with the Marines was a homecoming for Roger. I did see Roger on occasion, but not regularly. I caught up with him again in Saudi Arabia as we were getting ready to redeploy to the United States.

When I saw Roger, I couldn't believe my eyes. He was a mess. He was dirty and smelly and looked like an unmade bed. I exclaimed, "Roger, what in the world happened to you?" He explained that a little more than a month earlier the commanding general of the Marines at al-Jubail had ordered that his Marines decrease their water usage. A desalinization plant located on the Persian Gulf was used to provide water for the Marines at al-Jubail. This plant had a finite capacity for water production, and the Marines were using too much. The commanding general was intent on limiting the water used by his Marines. Following the general's directive, the water usage increased. The general therefore ordered that Marines limit themselves to two showers a week. The water usage continued to increase. So, the commanding general ordered that the showers be burned! This had occurred three weeks earlier, and my friend Roger hadn't had a shower since then.

✣

Shortly following my arrival in Baghdad, I determined that I would do everything possible to enhance the quality of life for the personnel assigned to the Coalition Provisional Authority. To that end, I had our team initiate programs that would make life in Baghdad a little more bearable. My chaplain assistants were all Navy chiefs. In the Navy, they are referred to as RPs (religious support specialists) and onboard ship are responsible for the ship's library. I put the RPs to work building a book exchange program, and we amassed a library of over five thousand books. Because the palace was a "tourist" stop for military and civilian personnel in Baghdad and the surrounding area, I got one of Saddam's thrones and placed it in the chapel so that soldiers could have their photographs taken sitting on it. But the pièce de résistance of our "quality of life" programs were the weekly trips that we organized to the ancient ruins at Babylon. Each week I was able to coordinate trips for between twenty and forty military and civilian personnel in the CPA.

Visiting the archeology site at Babylon was not only interesting in and of itself, but it was made more so for me because the 358th CA BDE had been attached to 1 MEF. That meant that every time we traveled to Camp Babylon I got to see friends with whom I'd been deployed in the past. It was like old home week! Life in support of the Marines was not easy, however. Looking at them reminded me of my friend Roger Ullman after he had gone without a shower for three weeks.

✣

Chaplain (Commander) Emilio "Felix" Marrero was the Command Chaplain for 1 MEF. He was an energetic fellow who had made the preservation of the ruins at Babylon his personal project. Since the Marines had encamped around the site and had established their perimeter with the ruins at the center, Chaplain Marrero had an easy time keeping a careful eye on this archeological treasure. He discovered some of the archeologists who had worked the site under Saddam's directive and "hired" them to give guided tours of the ruins to anyone who had access to Camp Babylon. This included U.S. and Coalition military personnel, as well as civilians assigned to the CPA.

The archeologists were all university educated and fluent in English. Each one had his or her area of special interest. Fatima, for example, was literate in cuneiform. I remember that we came across a brick that had an inscription by Nebuchadnezzar, and Fatima translated it on the spot. I also remember that she pronounced King Nebuchadnezzar's name in a way that was new to me. She said, "Neb-u [*u* as in the *oo* in *zoo*] chad [like the country *Chad*] ne [as in *nay*] zar [*czar*]." Ibrahim and the three or four other archeologists each had their own insights on the dig at Babylon and the history of the Babylonian Empire. Each time I visited the site and took the tour I tried to get into a group with a different archeologist so I could learn their perspective on Babylon.

During the tour, one saw the tell that had been the Tower of Babel. One was taken to a location where Daniel's lion den might have been located. The tour included stepping into the room where the Scriptures of Israel in the Book of Daniel tell us the writing appeared on the wall. That is the same room where Alexander the Great died. There was, however, one notable omission during the tour of the ruins at Babylon. We never saw the sight of the "Hanging Gardens," one of the Seven Wonders of the Ancient World. All our Iraqi archeologists were in agreement that the "Hanging Gardens" were not located at Babylon. Some were convinced that they were located at the "summer palace" of Nebuchadnezzar.

The ancient Babylonians were expert at glazing bricks. Throughout the ruins one could find shards of brick and pottery that were so rich in color that one could never have imagined them to be twenty-five hundred years old. One of the most difficult things to do after finding a piece of brick or pottery was to put it back on the ground instead of in one's pocket. Even shards of pottery are considered antiquities, and it is a violation of general orders to remove them from the site. Military personnel discovered in the possession of antiquities are punishable under the UCMJ (Uniform Code of Military Justice).

Chaplain Marrero had a real vision for the restoration of the museum and gift shop and managed to secure monies to reestablish both. Unfortunately, neither he nor I stayed in Iraq long enough to see the completion of these projects.

✢

I received a phone call from Marian, the DVB (Distinguished Visitor Bureau) chief on 02 September informing me of two things. First, the Secretary of Defense (SECDEF) would be visiting Iraq on 06 September and wanted to tour the ruins of ancient Babylon. Second, since 1 MEF was in the process of rotating out of Iraq and would be gone before he arrived, I was now the SME (subject matter expert) on Babylon! The next day I received two e-mails, both requesting a short biography of me for Donald Rumsfeld's read-ahead packet. One of these came from Marian and the other from a friend of mine in the Chief of Chaplains office in the Pentagon. It was evident that everyone was getting spun up over the SECDEF's visit.

I spent a great deal of time between the second and sixth of September becoming the SME on ancient Babylon that I was touted to be. I studied everything that I could get my hands on and organized an outline of the topics I wanted to cover that would coincide with the route I planned to take through the ruins. There were a couple of things that I found fascinating about the ancient Babylonians. They loved higher mathematics and for entertainment solved math problems—and it had been a struggle for me just to pass algebra! The other thing that I found extremely interesting was their religious culture.

The primary god of the Babylonians was Marduk. In fact, Babylon boasted more than eleven hundred temples dedicated to various gods. It appears that each time they conquered a foreign land they transported the gods of that land back to Babylon. Apparently they did not want to offend any of the gods and worshipped them all. Marduk, however, was chief among them and the patron god of Babylon. The thing that struck me about Marduk was the similarity he bore to the God of Abraham, Isaac, and Jacob. I never fully understood why, in the Book of Daniel, King Nebuchadnezzar is more or less friendly to his captives the Jews and respectful of the God of Israel. The answer is, I believe, that the one true God of the Jews and Marduk share a number of important attributes. Marduk was the god who brought order out of chaos. He was a god of compassion who sought justice. No wonder some of the Jewish captives rose to positions of prominence within Nebuchadnezzar's court.

✢

I was instructed to meet the SECDEF's entourage at Camp Victory located beside BIAP (Baghdad International Airport) on the morning of 06 September. We would then be flown to Babylon for the tour. I would be traveling in the press corps helicopter. What I did not know at the time was that we would have another stop prior to our arrival at Babylon. Not far from al-Hillah is a mass gravesite of Iraqis who had been murdered in one of Saddam's purges. We exited the helicopters and were driven to a knoll overlooking a vast area where thousands of Iraqi men, women, and children had been shot and buried. Atop the graves hundreds of clear plastic bags had been pegged to the ground, each containing items recovered from the bodies. These bags contained bits of clothing and other personal items. They were placed there in the hope that those visiting the site and looking for loved ones who may have disappeared could identify the dead by means of their personal effects. As the SECDEF spoke to the assembled press corps and others who were present, dozens of Iraqis combed the site looking at the personal items in the bags with the hope of locating a missing loved one. In an instant, my role as SME for ancient Babylon was placed in its proper perspective.

Not only had Donald Rumsfeld done his "homework" on me by reviewing my bio in his read-ahead packet, I had done my homework on him. I have a friend who had worshipped in the same congregation with him and his wife. So, when he began to engage me in conversation about my work and background, I started talking to him about my read-ahead concerning him. The tour of ancient Babylon lasted about forty-five minutes. I was struck by how visiting the ruins made wide-eyed kids out of us all. Donald Rumsfeld wasn't the Secretary of Defense for those forty-five minutes; he was a tourist on the pilgrimage of a lifetime. Following the tour, LTG Craddock pulled me aside and handed me one of the SECDEF's coins. There is a long tradition in the military of presenting coins to individuals as an award for a job well done. Commanders in the rank of LTC or higher generally have a coin to present individuals who have performed well. In Kuwait, while serving as the command chaplain for the 377th Theater Support Command, I too had a coin designed and manufactured for presentation to those who were instrumental in providing religious support. The SECDEF's coin was about two inches in diameter with a light blue enameled flag in the center. A navy blue enameled border with "Donald Rumsfeld Secretary of Defense" circled the edge of it.

It was a privilege for me to escort the SECDEF through the ruins of Babylon and receive his coin. My only regret is that Chaplain Marrero, who had done all of the work to coordinate visits at Babylon, had not been able to be commended by Mr. Rumsfeld for his outstanding work.

Throughout the ruins at ancient Babylon one can find bricks containing cuneiform writing with an inscription to the great King Nebuchadnezzar. Not to be outdone by Nebuchadnezzar, who conquered all of Mesopotamia and what surrounded it, Saddam Hussein rebuilt the façade of Babylon on the ancient foundations. Embedded in the walls of the new construction one easily discovers bricks inscribed in Arabic honoring the great twentieth-century monarch of Mesopotamia, Saddam Hussein!

Chapter 10

Lieutenant Colonel Chad Buehring

U.S. Army

The U.S. Army goes to war by doctrine. That doctrine is an ever-changing, ever-maturing, ever-evolving, and living series of tenets constructed to ensure success on the battlefield. When I was accessioned into the Army in 1982, the doctrine by which we fought was entitled "AirLand Battle." Some of the tenets of this doctrine were unity of command, agility, surprise, economy of force, and synchronization. Every basic officer course had a block of instruction to instill this doctrine into its junior leaders. The Chaplain Officer Basic Course (CHOBC—pronounced *cho-bic*) was no exception. If I recall correctly, we received a two- or three-day period of instruction covering the tenets of AirLand Battle.

The fact of the matter is that I discovered the tenants of AirLand Battle to be useful, not only in comprehending the Army's doctrine for war but also in my civilian work. After all, what organization can't be more effective when it possesses unity of command, synchronization, and agility?

Today's U.S. military doctrine might be described as "battle space shaping." It is a doctrine that is joint in nature (i.e., involving highly coordinated maneuver elements of the Army, Navy, Air Force, Marines, and Coast Guard) and integrates civilian contractors for mission success. This doctrine is NET Centric (i.e., relying upon electronic information systems) and conducts "Effect-Based Operations."

The Al-Rasheed Hotel became the primary residence for personnel assigned to the Coalition Provisional Authority in July of 2003. The hotel is a fourteen-story edifice that contains various shops, restaurants, and a grand ballroom. It is familiar to most people because it was used as the headquarters for the international press corps during Desert Storm and it was from that location that the bombardment of Baghdad was captured nightly. The Al-Rasheed is located about a mile and half away from the presidential palace. It is situated on the edge of the "Green Zone." I never referred to it as the Green Zone because of all the mortars and rockets that fell within it regularly. I dubbed it the "Amber Zone," which more appropriately reflected the reality of the situation there.

Following the first Gulf War, Saddam demanded that the marble floor in the grand entrance be removed and a new floor set in its place. This new floor contained either a mosaic or painted likeness of President George Bush, thus ensuring that all visitors to the hotel would walk on the American president both upon entering and leaving the hotel. Prior to our move from the palace into the hotel, the picture was removed and a new floor devoid of the Bush likeness placed in its stead. Those of us in the rank of colonel were given rooms on the fourteenth floor. I was given a suite of three rooms overlooking the Baghdad zoo, the Iraqi memorial to their unknown soldier, and the parade field. The parade field is unique in that two crossed swords standing many stories high are situated at either end of the grounds. These crossed swords were constructed from the helmets of Iranian soldiers killed during the Iran-Iraq War.

✣

It may be surprising to some to learn that the U.S. military goes to war by doctrine. It may be even more surprising to learn that the U.S. Army has a mission statement. The Army's mission statement is "Relevant and Ready Land Power in Service to the Nation." I would not have known this fact had it not been for a Memorial Day prayer breakfast that I organized in 2007 at Camp Arifjan, Kuwait. Prayer breakfasts are a favorite program of chaplains in the Army. Generally a space is set aside in the dining facility for people to gather and eat together. After breakfast comes a program that contains prayers, hymns and choirs, scriptural readings, and a guest speaker. I had invited Chaplain (Brigadier General) Douglas Lee to come to Kuwait and address us for this important remembrance. Chaplain Lee is the Assistant Chief of Chaplains for Mobilization and Readiness. He began his remarks by asking those present what the Army's mission statement is. There was not one individual present who could answer his question. To be fair, however, he did exempt LTG Whitcomb, Third Army Commander, and the Third Army deputy commander from responding to his question. I am certain that he did this to ensure that they would not be embarrassed. I would be surprised if either of them was aware of the Army's mission statement but am happy to give them the benefit of the doubt.

One might expect that any Army that has a mission statement and goes to war by doctrine might have soldiers who are very familiar with their particular responsibilities. Army unit ministry teams (i.e., a chaplain and a chaplain assistant) also conduct their mission essential tasks by doctrine. Moreover, UMTs have what I refer to as three ministry imperatives. These are to "nurture the living, care for the dying, and honor the dead." I see these imperatives as the sacred trust given to chaplains and chaplain assistants that are nonnegotiable. If UMTs are not nurturing the living, caring for the dying, and honoring the dead, then they are not carrying out their most important duty.

It was a real treat for the members of the Coalition Provisional Authority to move into the Al-Rasheed Hotel. I personally enjoyed not having to live in the same building where I worked. I also enjoyed the fact that from time to time I could take a break from eating in the dining facility and have an Arab meal at one of the restaurants in the hotel. Since I am fond of lamb, any Arab restaurant is going to be a treat for me. Following dinner the first time we ate in the hotel, eight of us were brought dessert menus. Wow, this certainly was a treat! The menu contained all sorts of ice cream dishes, each with its own name. One was the "Ali Baba" and another the "Aladdin." Each of these had different kinds of ice cream with different toppings. We must have taken twenty minutes to review the menu before all of us could make up our minds as to which desert we wanted. Finally, we gave our dessert order. I think that I ordered something with three various ice creams and chocolate topping. When the waiter returned with our desserts, they were all the same: vanilla ice cream with chocolate sauce. So much for the time spent poring over the dessert menu!

An initial determination had been made that the Al-Rasheed Hotel would be on the Baghdad power grid. It would be subject, therefore, to the same energy issues faced by all Iraqis living in Baghdad. It must be understood that one of the policy changes made by the Coalition Provisional Authority was that all Iraqis would share equally in the national power supply. During the reign of Saddam, Baghdad was always given preference for electrical power. Other parts of the country would go without power in order to supply Baghdad. When the CPA took over control of the electrical grid, it appeared to the residents of Baghdad and also to the international media that the electrical supply had gotten much worse than under Saddam. In point of fact, the electrical system was about the same. It was just everyone was sharing equally in the energy produced or lack thereof. The aim of the CPA was to provide power twelve hours daily for all Iraqis. One of my Iraqi friends joked with me; "You Americans have got your energy policy half right. You have it working perfectly during the twelve hours we go without power. It is the twelve hours that we are to receive power that you can't seem to manage properly!" This statement was shared with me as good-natured kidding, but one could read the frustration and sense of hopelessness between the lines.

Power outages at the Al-Rasheed Hotel were commonplace. Any time, day or might, one was apt to lose electricity. This was particularly distressful on stinking hot days or early mornings when water pressure disappeared when one was bathing. Of course, I was always cognizant of the fact that thousands of U.S. military personnel were continually without power and didn't have water for bathing or air conditioning on hot nights. It tempered my frustration with the Baghdad power grid.

One of the outlets in all the Al-Rasheed rooms worked even during power outages. Saddam had built into the hotel a secret monitoring system for spying on his "guests." His secret police wanted to know what everyone in the hotel was up to all the time. Therefore, a separate power supply was provided within the hotel itself. This power supply supported hidden cameras and an outlet beneath the writing desks in each room. Prior to our moving into the hotel, the hidden cameras were removed.

My biggest difficulty due to the power supply came on the evening of 23 June on my return to the hotel after work. I was in the elevator with two other individuals when the power went out. One of them had been telling us the story of her last ride on the elevator. Apparently the power had gone out on that occasion as well. I made a mental note not to share the elevator with her again! We were trapped between the twelfth and thirteenth floors with no escape. Since power outages could last for hours or days, it was cause for concern. I certainly didn't want to spend a few days trapped in an elevator in the dark and without food or water. Luckily, one of the bellboys at the hotel called up to the elevator cars to see if anyone was trapped. And just as we were being rescued a few minutes later, the power came back on and we made it to our floors.

U.S. military personnel in combat zones are entitled to "imminent danger pay." This is additional pay received for being in harm's way. Following my excursion on the Al-Rasheed elevator, I quipped that it was the first time I felt I'd earned that entitlement. Little did I realize I'd be given many more opportunities to qualify for imminent danger pay.

It wasn't too long after this power outage that a determination was made that the Al-Rasheed Hotel needed to have its own power supply and not be dependant on the Baghdad power grid. Two huge electrical generators were placed outside the hotel, and electricity was supplied almost without interruption.

✝

I served with the 358th Civil Affairs Brigade in the Bosnia peacekeeping mission from June of 1998 until February of 1999. Bosnia was also considered an imminent danger zone, and we were entitled to imminent danger pay. U.S. military personnel deployed to danger zones are also generally entitled to tax exclusion status. Imminent danger pay and the tax exclusion privilege are extended to service personnel if one spends as little as one day in the entitlement zone. It should come as no surprise to learn, therefore, that enterprising military personnel living just outside the imminent danger and tax exclusion zone found creative reasons for visiting Bosnia on a regular basis. While we were in Bosnia, all sorts of military personnel from Hungary showed up on the last day of the month for missions that extended into the first day of the following month. They were thus entitled to the tax exemption and imminent danger pay for two months time. It also goes without saying that those of us who were in harm's way day in and day out were incensed by this abuse.

The Third Army Command in Kuwait established a policy that prohibited general officers from visiting Kuwait at the end of a month and overlapping into the following month. I have no doubt that this policy was aimed at correcting the tax exclusion and imminent danger pay abuses that were so prevalent in Bosnia. This policy also guarded against the perception that high-ranking officers were using their privileged positions to cheat the U.S. taxpayer.

It was my intention to conduct prayer breakfasts at two of the bases in Kuwait at the end of May and beginning of June 2007 to fulfill my duty as chaplain to honor the dead. Two days were required for this mission because the camps were very distant from each other and travel did not permit the prayer breakfasts to be conducted on the same day. I had invited Chaplain (Brigadier General) Lee to visit Kuwait from the United States because I believed that his presence would add an air of importance and dignity to these events. I also believed that his presence would highlight for all U.S. service personnel the necessity of honoring our dead in the most prestigious manner possible. It was my intention to conduct prayer breakfasts at Camp Arifjan and also at Camp Buehring.

✝

Twenty-seven rockets struck the Al-Rasheed Hotel on the twenty-sixth of October 2003 at about 0600 hours. One soldier was killed during the attack. His name was Chad Buehring, and he was a Special Forces lieutenant colonel who worked for the Coalition in the Office of Strategic Communications. Almost immediately following the attack, I was instructed by Ambassador Bremer to visit the members of the STRATCOM team as they grieved the death of LTC Buehring. It quickly became evident to me that he had been well respected, even beloved by his coworkers. It was also evident that they would need to work through their grief at his death and their shock at being the target of attack at the Al-Rasheed Hotel. In the days ahead, I conducted individual counseling, participated in a critical incident stress debrief, and planned Chad's memorial service with them.

The evening of the attack on the Al-Rasheed Hotel everyone living there was required to collect some of their belongings and move to other locations for billeting. It was hoped that this move would be temporary and that we would be permitted to return to the Al-Rasheed after repairs were completed. It soon became evident, however, that we would never return to the Al-Rasheed and that we would have to clear all of our belongings from our rooms.

I returned to my room a few days after the attack to pack my belongings and move out. The hotel was a mess. Shattered glass was everywhere, the elevators were inoperable, and the smell of explosives and charred wood hung in the air. After I packed up my things, I determined to walk down to the eleventh floor so that I could stand in Chad's room and pray for the repose of his soul and for comfort for his wife and children. Since there was no electricity, I took my flashlight with me. I stopped outside his room, put down my duffel bags and stepped inside. The room was a shambles. Ceiling tiles hung from above, wires protruded from the wall, and water from the sprinkler system had soaked everything. The room smelled musty and dank. I stepped in, bowed my head, and prayed. Tears welled up in my eyes not simply because of Chad's death or even because of his family's grief, but because at that moment it felt to me as if I was standing in a sacred place where, in the midst of death, I had come seeking God.

The prayer breakfasts in Kuwait at the time of Memorial Day were far more than a program for which I was responsible. Early in my deployment to Kuwait I learned about Camp Buehring. It is the staging point for U.S. military personnel traveling into Iraq. I was convinced that it was too coincidental for there to be two Buehrings and that this camp must be named for LTC Chad Buehring. Upon my first visit to the camp, I stopped just inside the control point and saw a memorial to him. These Memorial Day prayer breakfasts were personal, and I was more determined than ever to fulfill the Chaplain Corps imperatives. I would honor the dead, especially LTC Chad Buehring. I would see to it that he was remembered at the camp bearing his name.

Bringing a general officer or anyone into theater is a process that requires four or five months. The process requires an invitation from a sponsoring commander. It requires a written justification. It also requires clearances and approval from all superior headquarters. Bringing a chaplain into theater requires the additional obligation of keeping the "chaplain chain of command" informed.

The easiest part of the process for me was writing the justification for bring CH (BG) Lee to Kuwait. He was coming to assist me in performing the most sacred mission the Army has, namely, honoring its war dead. Not only would we be honoring those who had died in the service of our nation, but we would also be honoring one for whom a camp within our area of operations had been named. Who in their right mind could object?

Answer: everyone!

It was unbelievable to me that I received resistance from every echelon above me. I had to rewrite my justification of Chaplain Lee's visit no less than five times. I had to explain to the military why it is imperative that we honor our war dead and have Chaplain Lee cross the May–June monthly boundary. I had to explain that he also is a reserve officer and that his tax exclusion entitlement would only apply to a few days of service. He would not be receiving two whole months' tax exclusion. Following three months of justification and rejustification for his visit, approval was given for him to come, and he was granted clearance to enter Kuwait. Hurray! Exceptions to policy can be granted for rational, well-thought-out, and necessary events. He'd be coming, and we would adequately and honorably remember Chad Buehring along with all of our war dead.

Chaplain Lee was scheduled to depart the United States on the Monday evening of Memorial Day weekend and arrive on Tuesday at the Kuwait City International Airport. On the Thursday immediately preceding Memorial Day weekend, the Third Army Commander was briefed on CH Lee's visit and pulled the plug on his entry into Kuwait. I was informed of this action that afternoon and couldn't believe my ears. Why had the individual who was the ultimate decision maker not been informed earlier? Months of planning had gone down the drain. Airline tickets had been purchased and itineraries planned. The Army's Assistant Chief of Chaplains had arranged his schedule to aid us in honoring our war dead. Thankfully, the individual who informed me of LTG Whitcomb's action had also suggested that if my Commanding General spoke to LTC Whitcomb, CH Lee might be permitted to come to Kuwait.

I rushed in to speak with MG Robinson. He in turn visited LTG Whitcomb, and the visit was turned back on.

There are not too many things I'm willing to die in a ditch for as a senior Army chaplain. Generally, I choose my battles carefully. I don't choose to go toe to toe with superior officers and the staffs of higher echelon headquarters. However, I become more than somewhat indignant when military bureaucrats stand in the way of my sacred duty as a chaplain in honoring our war dead. It is at moments like these that I am unwilling to accept no as the final answer.

CH (BG) Lee was an absolutely fantastic speaker. He began with the Army's mission statement, "Relevant and Ready Land Power in Service to the Nation," and then spoke of the notion of service to our country and asked us to consider that we are called the armed services for a reason. When he sat back down at the table, where he was seated with LTC Whitcomb and the deputy Third Army commander, LTC Whitcomb leaned over to him and whispered in his ear, "I'm certainly happy we let you come into Kuwait!"

Part of the mission of an Army chaplain is to nurture the living, care for the dying, and honor the dead. It is more than a responsibility; it is a sacred trust.

What surprises me, however, is how hard it sometimes is in the military to do what I believe ought to be self-evident to everyone.

Chapter 11

Chaplain (Major) Ken Sorenson

U.S. Army

A young Marine was brought to my office by his staff sergeant. The staff sergeant had called me earlier in the day informing me that he had a Marine who was talking about killing himself and wanted to know if I'd be willing to talk with his lance corporal. I, of course, agreed. I began my chat with the lance corporal by asking if his staff sergeant was correct in telling me that he wanted to kill himself. "Yes," he replied, "I don't want to live any longer." When I asked him why he wanted to kill himself, he informed me that he had just received news that his brother had committed suicide.

Chaplains have the mission for suicide prevention in the U.S. Army. All chaplains are trained in suicide prevention and mitigation. On top of that, all chaplains are required to give yearly briefs to the soldiers in their commands regarding the symptoms of suicide, proper verbal responses to someone contemplating suicide, and the correct action to be taken. Every soldier deployed to the theater of operations in Iraq, Afghanistan, and Kuwait is required to receive a suicide prevention brief prior to their R&R and again prior to their redeployment. I conducted suicide prevention briefs in Baghdad three times a week for individuals leaving theater. I was fully aware that individuals who have a family history of suicide are more apt to have suicidal ideation than others.

I spoke to this young lance corporal for over an hour. I then asked if it would be all right for me to make an appointment for him to see a psychiatrist at the 113rd Combat Stress Detachment. He agreed, and I left him to walk fifteen feet down the hallway to the medics' office and set up the appointment. If I've said it once, I've said it a thousand times: "NEVER LEAVE A SUICIDAL PERSON ALONE!" What in the world was I thinking? When I returned to the office, I saw something I'd missed when his staff sergeant dropped him off with me. Under his blouse, strapped to his belt, there was a holster with a pistol! What in the world was he doing with a gun? I thank my lucky stars that this lance corporal didn't kill himself in the few minutes I was out of the office. His staff sergeant and I broke the first two cardinal rules in responding to someone who is contemplating suicide. His sergeant didn't take his weapon from him, and I left him alone.

The Army has a master plan for the mobilization and deployment of its units. The plan has been tailored to both the active and reserve components. According to the plan, units on the "active" side of the house come into a zone for deployment every three years. This means, in effect, that soldiers who serve in the regular Army have the possibility of being deployed once every three years. The fact that active component units come into the zone for possible deployment does not necessarily mean that they will be deployed; it means that they may be deployed. Reserve component units, to include the National Guard and Army Reserve, come into a zone for possible mobilization and deployment every five years. Again, this does not necessarily mean that those units will be deployed; it merely means that those units may be deployed. Soldiers serving in the Guard and Reserve have the possibility of being deployed once every five years. This is the master plan, the grand scheme for the deployment of U.S. Army units.

The difficulty with this master plan lies not so much with the plan itself as with the execution of the plan. The fatal flaw for active component soldiers is that many of the Army's combat units are deploying for more than a year at a time and then deploying again with less than a two-year respite. The actual cycle for some units is fifteen months deployed and twelve months at home. That means soldiers can expect to be deployed for two and a half out of every three and a half years they serve in the regular Army. There are literally thousands of U.S. Army personnel who have been deployed three or four times since 2002. During my year at Camp Arifjan, I met soldiers in a particular unit who were deployed on a six-month cycle of rotations between Kuwait and the United States. When I first spoke with one of these soldiers, the six-month rotation schedule sounded pretty good to me. Soldiers would get to see their families for half of each year. Then I learned that the soldier with whom I was speaking had been away from home for Christmas (and probably Thanksgiving) for the past five years!

The fatal flaw for the reserve component is twofold. The reserve component does not have the troop strength to support a five-year cycle for unit deployment. And its soldiers are "citizen warriors." Can you imagine applying for a job and informing your potential employer that you'll only be available for work 80 percent of the time?

The deployment of Reserve soldiers restricts their call-up to a two-year maximum for the same contingency operation within a five-year window. Soldiers who have served at least one year of mobilization for a particular operation cannot be recalled to active duty in support of that same contingency operation without signing a waiver agreeing to do so. Those of us who had been deployed in the past knew that the five-year rotation for reserve component units was not going to work. There simply were not enough soldiers to fill all the units coming into consideration for mobilization. So, the Army Reserve resolved its shortfall by "resetting the clock." The grand scheme of units coming into the zone for possible deployment erased the time that individual reservists had spent mobilized and deployed since 2002. If one returned just six months ago from a two-year deployment, it didn't matter: the clock has been reset. During previous contingency operations, the Army simply changed the name of the operation. A reservist can't be deployed twice within a five-year window for the same contingency, so let's rename the operation!

The most important lesson to learn when serving in the Army is that the Army always fills its needs. Some years ago, I was speaking with my CG (Commanding General), who was spun up over the fact that many soldiers being mobilized and deployed couldn't even pass a PT (physical training) test. He believed that the Army had a duty to send physically capable soldiers "down range." I said to him, "Sir, remember that the Army always fills its needs. It doesn't matter what policies are broken. It doesn't matter if soldiers don't meet all the requirements. All that matters is that the Army fills its needs!" I thought everyone in the Army already had this figured out. The Army always does whatever is necessary to do to complete the mission. My observation was, however, an epiphany for my CG.

✠

Prior to my first suicide prevention brief in Baghdad, I thought it would be a good idea to talk to a few commanders to see what I could learn through their experience in dealing with suicidal soldiers. One colonel shared this story with me from his years as a battalion commander.

A young troop was brought to him because this soldier had been talking about suicide. The commander sat this soldier down in his office and said, "I understand that you're thinking of killing yourself. Why?"

The soldier responded, "Sir, I am five hundred dollars behind in the payment of debts and I can't think of any way to resolve this crisis."

Much to the commander's credit, he simply pulled out his checkbook, wrote out a check for $500, and handed it to the soldier saying, "Here, take this, we'll figure out how you can repay me later."

Wherever I gave suicide prevention briefs, I always used this story. I attempted to explain we have already confronted and resolved many issues in our lives that may have life-and-death consequences for others. We merely need to keep alert to the symptoms of suicidal behavior and respond appropriately. I also suggested that what may not be a big deal for us can be a very big deal to someone else.

✣

Chaplain (Major) Ken Sorenson was the 1st AD, 2nd BCT (1st Armor Division, 2nd Brigade Combat Team) chaplain. His commander's AOR (area of responsibility) included the Green Zone and parts of Sadr City. CH Sorenson regularly visited the battalion chaplains working under his supervision. Every now and again he would show up at the palace for a chat. He always came in to see me looking worn out and filthy. He was always out visiting troops, chaplains, or Muslim religious leaders in Sadr City for hours on end, wearing full "battle rattle" in temperatures well over one hundred and twenty degrees. In spite of it, he was the most upbeat, positive, enthusiastic chaplain I have ever encountered. He always brightened my day, and I was happy when I could offer him a cold drink of water (it is amazing how bad hot water tastes on a stinking hot day in the desert).

CH Sorenson was in Iraq with the 1st AD for about six months. The reason he was only to be in the desert for six months was because he was being transferred to the 1st CAV (1st Cavalry Division) in Ft. Hood, Texas. The unfortunate part about his transfer is that it meant he'd be returning to Iraq for a year in the very near future. The active component does not make allowances for soldiers who have just been transferred into a new command even if those soldiers have just arrived from a deployed unit.

✣

It may appear strange that the Army insists that soldiers returning from deployment be required to receive suicide prevention briefs from a chaplain. Aren't soldiers happy to be going home? Aren't they looking forward to getting out of the desert? Why in the world does the Army need do anything except thank them and send them on their way rejoicing? Three answers to these questions spring to mind immediately. Many returning veterans experience a loss of identity, a loss of family, and a loss of job (job loss is a Reserve phenomenon). The loss that is experienced is more than some individuals can handle. The suicide rate in the Army prior to the deployment of soldiers into the theater of operations in Iraq, Afghanistan, and Kuwait was thirteen per hundred thousand per year. The suicide rate in the Army has risen to seventeen per hundred thousand per year. Commanders at every echelon within the Army want to reverse the trend of soldier suicides.

Imagine for a moment a twenty-four-year-old man or woman serving in Iraq. That individual may be responsible for millions of dollars in equipment. He or she may be responsible for the lives of seven other members of his or her squad. That person may manage a program for the training of hundreds of Iraqi police. The level of responsibility for young military personnel deployed to a combat zone is extraordinary. When they complete their year of service, to what do they return? Perhaps they come home to a menial job with no authority and virtually no responsibility. A few months ago these individuals were making life-and-death decisions for a combat team. Now they are spending their days sweeping floors or flipping burgers. The loss of identity upon redeployment can be significant, not only for soldiers who return to the civilian sector but even for those who remain in the Army. Life in garrison does not carry with it the same level of meaning as life on the streets of Baghdad.

Returning soldiers often experience a loss of family. The divorce rate in the Army is negatively impacted by the continuous cycle of mobilization and deployment. But the loss of family is not just about divorce rates in the military. The sense of a loss of family also accompanies one as he or she leaves the people with whom that person has been deployed. Soldiers are on the go 24/7 (twenty-four hours a day, seven days a week) when deployed. One is always active and surrounded by a team of soldiers who become one's "family" away from home. When one leaves the combat theater, one also leaves one's family.

Job loss is also significant for deployed soldiers. The United States has laws protecting military members who mobilize and deploy in support of the Global War on Terrorism. The Uniformed Services Employment and Reemployment Rights Act (USERRA) was established in 2004 to assist returning military personnel. Nevertheless, all laws have loopholes, and a substantial number of military personnel lose jobs upon their return home. Because of the "separation of church and state," workers employed by religious institutions find themselves at the mercy of their employers.

During mobilization and deployment, I lost two part-time positions. Ironically enough, the first of these was my Army Reserve job! I was sitting in my office in Baghdad catching up with the latest bulletins from the Command Chaplain of the Army Reserve. As I was reading along, I happened to notice that my Command Chaplain position at Ft. Devens, Massachusetts, was being advertised. I was a little chagrined because I had almost completed my deployment and was ready to return home. Was the Army "firing" me during my deployment? What's up with that? I immediately dropped a note off to CH (MAJ) Muldrow, my assistant at the 94th Regional Readiness Command. He didn't know a thing about this and was shocked at what I told him. Someone had attempted to make certain that I didn't have a Reserve position when I returned home. Fortunately, I was able to resolve this issue prior to my return home and did retain my command chaplain position.

The second of my part-time positions was with an organization in the Episcopal Church whose intent is to develop clergy wellness. During the tenure of my mobilization and following one of our team seminars, I received a phone call from my team leader informing me that she was dropping me from her team. I was surprised by this revelation in light of the fact that the team leader had always praised my presentations and work on the team. I was informed that the decision had already been made and my input was not required. I was not able to head off this job loss as I had my Reserve position. USERRA does not protect everyone who serves in the Global War on Terrorism. Many soldiers lose their jobs while deployed with the military. Chaplains, for example, do not enjoy the protection that federal law extends to those working in secular employment.

The loss of identity, the loss of family, and the loss of job all contribute to the growing number of Army personnel who commit suicide each year. One of the roles of the chaplain is to help mitigate suicidal behavior in the Army.

✠

Specialist (SPC) Quintana—we called him "Q"—worked as a chaplain assistant for my good friend in Iraq CH (CPT) Stanton Trotter. CH Trotter and I worked together on a number of projects and conducted weekly services together at the palace. SPC "Q" was to be transferred to another unit upon his redeployment. As he and CH Trotter were leaving Baghdad, I jokingly told "Q" I looked forward to seeing him upon his return. He assured me that there was no chance of that happening. He'd already been in touch with his supervisor at the unit to which he was going. He had been guaranteed that he wouldn't have to turn around and come right back. Less than sixty days later SGT (Sergeant—he'd been promoted) "Q" stopped by my office in the palace to introduce me to his new chaplain!

CH (MAJ) Ken Sorenson returned to Baghdad a little more than a month before I was due to leave. He'd been home with his wife and family for less than six months and would now be away from them for at least another year. I was both sad and happy to see him. I was sad that he'd be separated from his family for another year. I was also saddened by the fact that the Army doesn't take better care of its soldiers. But I was happy to see CH Sorenson again. He always brightened my day with his upbeat spirit and positive attitude. He'd even brought the 1st CAV division chaplain with him for a courtesy call.

When I encounter military personnel in their Class "A" uniform, I quickly glance at their left shoulder and read their "résumé." All U.S. military personnel wear their ribbons or medals above the blouse pocket on the left side of their uniforms. The ribbons will let you know if that person has been to Iraq or Afghanistan, and they will let you know if that individual has been called to serve in the United States as part of the Global War on Terrorism. The ribbons will tell you a great deal about a particular individual and his or her experience in the military. In the Army, soldiers have one other identifying emblem on their uniform that is not shared by the other services, the "combat patch." A combat patch is a unit insignia worn on a soldier's right sleeve at the shoulder. It is the insignia of the unit in which a soldier has been deployed to a combat theater. The patch of the unit to which one is assigned is worn on the left sleeve, the combat patch on the right.

In the post-Vietnam era of the Army, fewer and fewer personnel had combat patches. In today's Army, it is commonplace for soldiers to have a combat patch because most have been deployed to a combat zone. Soldiers are entitled to wear any *one* of their combat patches on their uniform at a time. That is probably a good thing, because today's soldiers have been deployed to combat zones on numerous times. It would certainly look strange to see a soldier with a string of patches running down his or her right sleeve!

Chapter 12

Paul Voorhees

Saddam's former presidential palace in Baghdad was a beehive of activity. It seemed like someone of note was always visiting the palace. There were American politicians, reporters, sports figures, and entertainers. There were Iraqi religious leaders and politicos. There were ambassadors from the Coalition nations. There were also Christian missionaries from a number of nations. The palace was the "center of gravity" for the world during my time in Baghdad.

One morning at our staff meeting, the DVB (distinguished visitor bureau) chief announced that U.S. Senator Jim Bunning would visit the palace the following week. I asked, "You know who he is, don't you?"

"He's a U.S. Senator," the reply came.

"No, I mean you know who he 'really' is? He was a professional baseball player," I said. Following the meeting I returned to my office, went online, and found his baseball credentials. Jim Bunning is in the Baseball Hall of Fame. The fact that he was a U.S. Senator was purely coincidental! I used to watch him pitch for the Philadelphia Phillies as a youngster. I quickly returned to the DVB office and passed on the information I found online. The DVB chief asked if I'd like to meet Senator Bunning when he came to Baghdad.

A couple days later I was standing in a designated space right outside Ambassador Bremer's office when Jim Bunning came past with his entourage, which must have included at least thirty people. I was introduced to him as he walked past and got to say a few words about watching him pitch for the Phillies. His face lit up instantly. He and his entourage then exited the rotunda and took the hallway north; I headed south to my office. Suddenly, I heard his voice above the crowd as he strode down the hallway, "Hey, where's the chaplain?" I called back and said that I was returning to work. He raised his arm and waved to me as he walked away. I got the impression that baseball was one of his happiest memories and that it made his day to be reminded of it.

✢

The USO (United States Overseas) is a wonderful organization that is intent on serving military personnel. Most Americans are probably familiar with the

USO because major airports in the United States have USO rooms. These rooms are set aside for military personnel who are traveling and may need a place to relax, sleep, or have a bite to eat while in transit. Most Americans are also probably familiar with the USO from watching old footage of Bob Hope on tour during World War II, the Korean War, and the Vietnam War. It is the USO that entertains troops abroad. During my tour in Gitmo (Guantanamo Bay, Cuba), the USO sponsored a concert with Garth Brooks. When I was in Bosnia, Eagle Base had a huge German tent erected. These tents are called fess tents. A construction crew is required to set up the tent because of the girders. Fess tents are larger than a football field inside when completed. The first USO live entertainment in the fess tent was Hootie and the Blowfish. Following their concert, the fess tent became known as the Hootie Dome. The USO brought entertainers to Kuwait. The WWF wrestlers, cheerleaders from one of the NFL team, comedians, and various musical groups visited us during my year's deployment.

The Convention Center inside the Green Zone is located directly across the street from the Al-Rasheed Hotel. It has served as the venue for press conferences and the trial of Saddam Hussein. It was the perfect location for the USO to stage entertainment. The first USO performers to appear on stage at the Convention Centers were Drew Carey, "Mimi," and a crew of five or six others who accompanied them. It was a two-hour show of laughter for U.S. military personnel stationed in the Green Zone. I don't think I've laughed so hard in my life. It was the first break we all had from the tension of living and working in the Green Zone. The morning following the show the Green Zone received a mortar attack. I guess not everyone found Drew Carey's jokes about terrorists all that amusing!

The thing I did not know at the time was that the entertainers who place themselves in harm's way to provide shows for U.S. military personnel are not paid for their work. It is their gift to the troops.

✠

Major General (MG) Paul Eaton approached me in the palace one day because he had a mission he wanted me to undertake. He had served as the commander of Ft. Benning, Georgia, prior to coming Baghdad. There was a fellow who lived in Columbus who did a great deal for the soldiers stationed at Ft. Benning, and he wanted to come to Iraq and visit the soldiers. His name was Paul Voorhees, and he was the owner of Ranger Joe's, a military supply shop that provides products and services to soldiers and police officers. Everyone in the Army knows about Ranger Joe's, especially the Rangers with whom Paul has had long-lasting friendships. The U.S. Army Ranger school is located at Ft. Benning, and Ranger Joe's is just outside the garrison. If the Rangers need something that the Army doesn't provide through its supply system, Paul will get it for them. Paul Voorhees is one of only two civilians to be inducted into the Ranger Hall of Fame. This is especially noteworthy since Paul has never even served in the military.

Paul Voorhees wanted to come to Iraq, not as the supplier of equipment to soldiers but as a person of faith. He wanted to encourage and inspire soldiers, not sell them products. He was going to pay his own way and live outside the Green Zone. MG Eaton wanted me to coordinate Paul's visit and make certain that Paul had the opportunity to interact with soldiers.

✝

I was continually amazed to see the dignitaries and other VIPs who showed up at the palace from time to time. There was Senator Joe Biden and Senator John McCain. There were reporters and news correspondents. Scott Pelley, one of the anchors from *60 Minutes*, used my office for an interview with Ambassador Bremer, so I chatted with him for a while as his crew got the lights and cameras ready. One morning a friend of mine from STRATCOM (strategic communications) was accompanying Ted Koppel through the security checkpoint. She leaned over to me and said, "Go introduce yourself to him."

So I did, "Mr. Koppel, I'm Chaplain Frank Wismer, welcome to Baghdad."

The thing that amazed me the most, however, were the groups of Christian missionaries that came to Iraq to provide food and supplies to the hungry and needy. These groups would eventually find their way to the palace and into my office. I would meet with them and then give them an escorted tour of the palace and palace grounds.

I remember one group of missionaries who were almost all in their sixties and seventies. They had come to Baghdad for a couple of weeks and were living in the city. They were in the most dangerous place in the world and were out riding around the countryside without security personnel or protection. They were so convicted in their beliefs that placing themselves in danger was insignificant.

There was also a Danish Pentecostal missionary named Peter Anderson. I met Peter in the palace at lunch one day. He was there meeting with the Danish ambassador (I believe that the ambassador was Danish—I know that he was Scandinavian). Peter simply hired a driver and a car and traveled around Iraq unescorted. I ran into Peter a second time months later when he was back in Iraq meeting with Iraqi Christian clerics in Baghdad.

Finally, I remember another group from an Evangelical church in the United States who was visiting Baghdad led by their pastor. I served a congregation in Smyrna, Delaware, during the 1990s. One of the other clergy in town got the idea that we ought to have a revival in our community and invite the Rev. Clyde Dupin to lead it. Clyde is an evangelist who travels the world conducting revivals. The result of the suggestion about having a revival in Smyrna is that Clyde Dupin came to Delaware for a week to preach and teach.

The pastor of the Evangelical church that visited the palace was named Dupin. I asked him if he was any relation to the evangelist Clyde Dupin (I don't know why I had remembered the name Clyde Dupin after so many years). He informed me that Clyde was his father. I then went on to tell him about my brief association with his father.

✢

I have a suspicion that most individuals feel called to the ordained ministry because they want to become part of something that is life transforming. They want to make a positive difference in the world. I also suspect that most individuals don't become part of the ordained ministry because they are merely interested in perpetuating institutions. Now, I could be wrong; it could very well be that most people really got ordained because they want to raise money, coordinate property improvements and building maintenance, and attend potluck suppers, but I doubt it. We (the ordained) dedicated our lives to God and the religious life because our lives had been transformed by an encounter with the Holy. More than anything else we wanted to be part of God's transforming work in a dynamic community. Instead, we became inundated with meetings and conversations about enlarging congregational membership. Gradually, religious institutionalism replaced our quest for the dynamic presence of God in community. Little by little we began measuring our effectiveness by our bureaucratic status within the institution rather than by the transformed lives of those with whom we were living in community.

I will go out on a limb and make an observation regarding the individuals who came to visit Baghdad. Senator Jim Bunning of Kentucky ran for office because he believed that he could help transform lives for the better. Ted Koppel and Scott Pelley became newsmen to make a difference, to help improve the quality of life for others. Drew Carey and "Mimi" became comedians to bring a few moments of joy and laughter into the lives of those they entertained thereby improving our quality of life.

✢

Paul Voorhees traveled into Iraq by car along with a missionary friend, Lynn Releford, from Jordan. They lived in a hotel for a week and traveled back and forth to the Green Zone daily. I would meet them at the Assassin's Gate checkpoint and serve as their host each day. Paul chatted with all the soldiers he encountered. He was very much a celebrity to them because they all knew him by his picture on the Ranger Joe's catalog. It almost felt as if he was part of a USO tour and that I was sponsoring Santa Claus. All the soldiers loved Paul and enjoyed the opportunity to chat with him. The Ranger Joe's catalog was like a peek at Santa's workshop with every toy any soldier could imagine! Moreover, Paul has the stature and friendliness of a short version of Santa Claus. Paul conducted a prayer breakfast with an M.P. battalion, he ate MREs (meals ready to eat) with soldiers preparing for missions, and he had a kind fatherly word for everyone he encountered. When Paul and Lynn left Baghdad, they promised to send Bibles to me for those working at the Coalition Provisional Authority. Three months later, four hundred and fifty Bibles arrived for us. They were in both English and Arabic. They disappeared in no time at all. Just about everyone who visited my office wanted a Bible. The Iraqis were thrilled to have Bibles in Arabic.

Paul Voorhees was such a wonderful witness to the love of God and such a hit with the troops that I invited him to come to Kuwait during my tour there. Again, Paul paid his own way. He conducted prayer breakfasts and met with the soldiers. He shared God's love with them through his words and also by sharing their hardships. One might be led to suggest that Paul Voorhees only came to visit the troops for self-serving purposes. This was not the case at all. The Army, cognizant of conflicts of interest, limited Paul's visit to supporting the religious program and not advertising his business. His only gain was in being permitted to share his faith with others and witnessing the transforming effect of God in his life.

✝

I am not a harsh critic of the church. I am convinced that the church is the beautiful bride of Christ. If I look at the church from time to time and perceive it as ugly or unattractive, then I probably need to have my vision checked. After all, if Jesus sees his bride as lovely and I see it as flawed then whose vision is skewed? I am firmly convinced that the church is a lovely and beautiful bride. It is in the context of the church as a beautiful bride that I make this observation.

Every day in Baghdad is an issue of life and death. Every day in Iraq Christians, Muslims, and Jews are persecuted for their beliefs. Every day in theater some soldiers are grappling with the sobering reality that they have taken the life of another in combat. One soldier came to see me for counseling. He needed to speak with a chaplain because he had just killed three people. Was he going to hell? Every day one's friends are being killed or wounded. Every day one lives with getting shot at, IEDs, and incoming mortars. Every Sunday Christians have to decide whether going to worship is worth the price of getting blown up by a bomb or murdered by terrorists.

Many issues that are hotly debated within the church and are so much the center of religious dialogue in America just don't matter! They pale in comparison to the real issues of faith that are confronted by the Iraqi people and U.S. military personnel daily. To be truthful, the issues that were being debated in the church in America just seemed silly. From the perspective of my life in Baghdad, the religious debate in America might just as well have revolved around how many angels could dance on the head of a pin!

The best job, the absolute best job I have ever had in my life, was serving as a chaplain in Baghdad, Iraq. During my time in Baghdad, I was shot at, mortared, rocketed, and IEDed, but it was also the occasion for the fulfillment of my call to the ordained ministry. In Iraq, I had the opportunity to be part of a dynamic community that was witness to God's transforming power in the lives of God's people. It was in Baghdad that I rediscovered the heart and soul of ordained ministry. It was in the chaos of Baghdad that I was renewed in my ministry. There wasn't one day that I didn't look forward to going to work. There wasn't one day that was devoid of God's powerful presence. I would return to Baghdad in a heartbeat!

✝

Paul Voorhees and hundreds of individuals like him visited Iraq continually. Their presence was a testament to the action of God in God's world. Thousands of Americans back home supported the Iraqi people and the members of the Coalition Provisional Authority with cards, letters, boxes of goodies, religious material, and their prayers. They were to us the life-giving presence of God in the midst of death and destruction.

Some people may wonder how it is that I could find my ministry in a combat zone so life giving while I find the combative debate within the church so life threatening. It is certainly a question worth considering, not only for me, but for those who feel compelled to ask it.

Chapter 13

Carole Basri

I became an Army Chaplain in 1982. At that time, the future of the military chaplaincy was very much in doubt. Lawsuits had been filed against the government asserting that having chaplains in the military was tantamount to the establishment of religion and, therefore, unconstitutional. The Army Chaplain Corps and, I presume, the Chaplain Corps of the Navy and Air Force countered that military chaplains existed not for the establishment of religion but to ensure the "free exercise" of religion for all people within the uniformed services.

Chaplains in today's military must be cognizant of the fact that they do not exist to perpetuate the doctrinal positions of their major faith groups or denominations. Of course within the conduct of worship as prescribed by their particular religious tradition, Chaplains are free to preach and teach whatever beliefs they espouse. Military chaplains who will not ensure the free exercise of religion for all people place the continuation of the chaplaincy within the armed services at risk.

Iraq had a relatively vibrant Jewish community prior to the ascent of Saddam Hussein. Synagogues could be found scattered throughout the country, and the total Jewish population exceeded fifty thousand. Today in Iraq (that is, in 2003–2004) there are only twenty-eight Jews remaining. These are mostly elderly Iraqis who all live in Baghdad. One synagogue remains in the city but does not have the services of a rabbi. Moreover, when Chaplain and Rabbi (LTC) Ackerson visited Baghdad, the Jewish leaders were less than enthusiastic about the possibility of him conducting services at the synagogue during Passover. They prefer, and with good reason, to maintain a low profile.

The biography of Saddam Hussein will demonstrate that he was strongly influenced by two world leaders of the twentieth century: Joseph Stalin and Adolf Hitler. It should come as no surprise to learn, therefore, that Saddam did everything possible to dismantle the Jewish community in Iraq. A significant portion of Iraq's Jewish population eventually emigrated to Israel or the United States.

✠

Public Action, Inc. publishes an anti-Semitic (actually anti-Jewish, because Arabs are also Semites) rag that I discovered by accident when I was attempting to recollect some of the aspects of our religious support mission in Baghdad. I discovered, for instance, that the 9/11 hijack of airplanes and the attack on the World Trade Center and Pentagon was actually a Jewish plot. I was introduced to the "kindlier, gentler Timothy McVey."[1]I also learned something about the Episcopal Church heretofore unknown to me: "Of course Israel loves the 911 wars, and that is understandable. What could be more efficient than having American Gentiles wipe out Middle Eastern Gentiles who stand in the way of Jewish worldwide ambitions? What could be finer than handing over control of Arab oil wells to corporations controlled by Jews and Episcopalians?"[2]

What in the world could possibly inspire someone to suggest that Episcopalians are in league with Jews to grab control of Arab oil? I'm afraid the answer to this question is that I'm the culprit!

✠

Upon my arrival in Baghdad, I immediately set about coordinating the religious support mission for everyone assigned to the Coalition Provisional Authority and anyone else working within the palace. Actually, the religious support mission that I instituted extended beyond the CPA and the walls of the palace. U.S. contractors working within and without the Green Zone were included in the religious support plan. U.S. and foreign national military, diplomatic, and civilian personnel were supported by the religious support plan. And Iraqi nationals working for the CPA were incorporated in the plan. A few months after I arrived in Baghdad, a substantial religious support program was fully operational. That is, with one exception: we did not have any services for Jewish personnel assigned to the CPA or working in the Green Zone.

I was troubled by this fact and also by the fact that I could not seem to secure a Jewish lay leader to coordinate religious activities at the palace. Chaplains are required to see to the free exercise of religion. That mandate does not give one the latitude to conduct religious rites and ceremonies that are outside of one's denomination or major faith group. I am permitted, for example, to conduct the Episcopal Church's liturgy because I am an Episcopal priest. I may also conduct general Protestant worship and participate in ecumenical events. I may not lead Roman Catholic Mass or Muslim prayers or Jewish worship. It is for this reason that it is essential that military chaplains develop a religious support plan. Chaplains must be proactive in ensuring the free exercise of religion for all people. The gaping hole in my religious support plan is that it did not provide an opportunity for Jewish personnel to gather for prayer and worship.

Carole Basri was contracted by the CPA to provide legal assistance. She traveled back and forth between Baghdad and New York City frequently in the performance of her duties. I do not exactly remember how I first became introduced to her, but it may have been as a result of her concern regarding the lack of religious support for Jewish personnel assigned to the CPA. Not only was Carole a Jew, but she was a Jew of Iraqi origin. The wonderful thing about Carole is that she was intent on seeing that religious support was provided to the Jewish community at the palace and was willing to assist me in making this happen. In her trips back and forth to NYC, Carole brought Jewish prayer books and study materials. She also brought one item with her that I desperately wanted, and that was a menorah. I wanted the menorah so that I could use it during the season of Chanukah at the Christian services I was conducting in the palace.

Saddam's palace, especially the throne room, had been used for unspeakable acts of cruelty. It had been transformed into our chapel. It occurred to me that there was a direct parallel here between the purification and rededication of the temple in Jerusalem by the Maccabees and the purging of the vestiges of the Saddam regime from the palace. I wanted a menorah for Chanukah to symbolize the cleansing of the palace. What I expected was that Carole Basri would purchase one of those little menorahs with a small box of colorful candles. Instead, she contacted Oded Halahmy.

Oded was a Jew who had been born in Baghdad. He had emigrated to Israel in 1951 and lived there for many years. He was a world-renowned sculptor and well known in Israel for particular works of art. Carole approach Oded, and he consented to give to the CPA a menorah that he had made. The menorah was a beautiful piece of art containing symbols of Iraq in its composition. It was a copy of a gigantic menorah on display in Israel and valued at $5,000. When I received the menorah, I placed it in a prominent position in my office until it would be used at Chanukah.

The news of the celebration of Chanukah in Baghdad was quickly picked up by various Jewish news agencies in Israel and the United States. Oded Halahmy,

Carole Basri, and I were all mentioned in the article, and I was quoted: "This year Chanukah will not only be a remembrance of our salvation history, but the celebration of our shared experience in Baghdad." Halahmy was also quoted in the article: "The candelabrum is a symbol of peace and hope for the Jewish people. I wish the same thing for the Iraqi people."

Public Action, Inc., in the same publication that asserts that Jews and Episcopalians are attempting to take over control of the Arab oil supply, has this to say about me: "*The Jewish Week* informs us that America's head chaplain at Saddam's Palace is Col. Frank E. Wismer III. Wismer, whose surname appears in Jewish genealogy records, is an Episcopalian minister. He requested that a special menorah, belonging of [I believe that should be 'to'] the great-granddaughter of one of Baghdad's chief rabbis, be flown from New York to Baghdad for a Chanukah ceremony at Saddam's palace."

I believe that the reasoning behind the article of Public Action Inc. goes something like this: If Wismer wants a menorah for Chanukah in Baghdad, then he must certainly come from Jewish roots. Since he is an ordained Episcopal priest, then Episcopalians must certainly be in league with international Zionism to control Arab oil.

It is difficult to read news from Public Action Inc. with a straight face. I do not take anything they have said about my ancestors or me seriously. Actually, it is somewhat of an honor to be considered a threat by Public Action Inc. Any organization that sees Timothy McVey as an American hero is one that I am pleased stood opposed to my religious support plan for Baghdad.

However, to set the record straight, let me tell you what I know about the Wismer clan. The Wismer family came to the colonies in the eighteenth century and settled in what is now known as Wismer, Pennsylvania. I've never been to Wismer, but I understand it is a crossroads with a general store and not too much else. My great-great-grandfather was a Mennonite clergyman. I know this because there is a photo array of the family taken in the late 1800s. Everyone in the family is pictured except for my great-great-grandfather. It was against his religious beliefs to have his picture taken. My father and his parents were Lutherans. I ended up as an Episcopalian because it was my mother who took me to church and raised me in the faith. On my mother's side of the family, I am part of the clan MacFarland. My mother's father was named Clinton Rex MacFarland, and her brother Clinton Rex MacFarland, Jr. I believe that if I were ever to change my name, I'd choose to be another Clinton Rex MacFarland. It has an air of dignity to it. Here's my question for Public Action Inc.: if I did change my name to MacFarland, would I still be considered Jewish?

All new personnel who were assigned to the Coalition Provisional Authority were required to complete an orientation checklist that compelled them to visit my office. One day a young lieutenant was in processing, came to my office, and spied the menorah on the mantel. He was a Jew and was interested in services for Jewish personnel. I explained to him that we did not have a Jewish lay leader and could not conduct Jewish services. 1LT Carr agreed on the spot to become the coordinator for the Jewish religious support program at the palace. He immediately got to work contacting all the Jewish personnel that we could locate. He contacted the Army units in the Green Zone to see what Jewish personnel might be in those units. Most importantly, he began conducting Shabbat services on Friday evenings. I attended the first of these services to demonstrate my support for 1LT Carr and the fine work that he had done in organizing the Jewish community for worship.

Rabbi (LTC) Ackerson visited Baghdad on a number of occasions during my year there. The Army considers Jewish, Muslim, and Orthodox chaplains to be representatives of "high demand, low density" (HDLD) faith groups. This means that there is a high demand for the religious support given by these chaplains, but there are very few of them. Generally HDLD chaplains are assigned to an entire theater of operations or are brought into theater for the important religious observances of their faith. CH Mitch Ackerson was *the* rabbi for the Army in Kuwait and Iraq. His responsibilities may also have included Afghanistan. What struck me about CH Ackerson is that he simply got into his automobile with his chaplain assistant and drove, without escort, from Kuwait City to Baghdad. He was a man on a mission, and he did not permit anything to stand in the way of providing religious support throughout the theater. He was singularly courageous.

CH Ackerson had coordinated with the Army supply system to ensure that all items required for the Passover seder were on hand at the palace in Baghdad when he arrived. He would be with us for three days visiting with Jewish personnel and conducting seders in the evening. Like all chaplains, Rabbi Ackerson understood his mission to be the free exercise of religion for all people. His seder would be open to everyone interested in attending.

HDLD religious support requires careful planning. Military personnel will have to be provided transportation to the location of religious activities and then provided with meals and lodging. Lodging becomes a necessity for two reasons. First, travel at night generates its own security complications. Second, Orthodox Jews may not be out after dark on the Sabbath. All events held in the evening or late afternoon, for military personnel from outlying FOBs (forward operating bases), required that they spend the night at the palace.

CH Ackerson was an Orthodox Rabbi. This meant that the seder wouldn't be an "in and out" religious event. I had decided that I would support him in his work by attending one of the three seders he conducted. Three hours and forty-five minutes later we were finished. It was actually a very enlightening experience, and I very much enjoyed his teaching during the seder. Perhaps the most important thing of note is that about one hundred individuals attended the Seder nightly: Jews, Christians, and Muslims were all in attendance.

Many outsiders looking at the military fail to comprehend the fact that those chaplains in the armed services have statutory obligations to ensure the free exercise of religion for all people. Occasionally chaplains will forget this fact as well and believe that they are in the military to convert others to their religious persuasion.

In 1992, I spent three months at Guantanamo Bay, Cuba, as the ARFOR (Army Forces) command chaplain. I was responsible for overseeing the religious support program for all the Haitian migrants.

(As an aside, the word *migrant* was carefully selected to describe the Haitians at Gitmo because a "migrant" has no standing under U.S. and international law. The term *displaced civilian* or *detainee* is a title that is defined by law and dictates the rights and privileges of those individuals. Care was taken not to use any term that extended regulatory status to the Haitians at Guantanamo Bay.)

I noticed that the weekly chaplain report format I inherited contained the category "conversions." Furthermore, I noticed that when the figures were tallied each week there were generally more than twenty-four thousand conversions! Wait a minute, we only have about five thousand migrants in our camps. True, we have many coming and going daily, but probably not more than two thousand a week. How in the world do we have a weekly conversion number of twenty-four thousand?

So, at my weekly staff meeting with our chaplains and chaplain assistants I asked for an answer to this perplexing question. I was informed that there were two Unit Ministry Teams (UMTs) assigned to each of the five camps. One was a Roman Catholic team and the other was a Protestant team. In the morning, the Protestant team would go into the camp and convert all those who attended services. Since the only thing for Haitians to do at Gitmo was go to church services or programs provided by the chaplains, everyone was in church. Haiti, it is said, is 95 percent Roman Catholic and 100 percent voodoo. The fact that all of their congregants were being converted by the Protestants in the morning irritated the Roman Catholic chaplains. They visited the camps each afternoon and converted everyone back into Roman Catholics! That was the explanation for enormous number of conversions at Gitmo when I became the ARFOR command chaplain. I immediately put an end to the practice of conversion and instituted "truth in advertising" in my weekly chaplain report to the ARFOR commander.

I want to be very clear about one important point regarding religious support in the U.S. Army. That is, the religious program is not the chaplain's program—it is the commander's program. In matters of religious support, the chaplain serves as personal staff to the commander for the implementation of religious support. Funding for the religious support program in the Army is obtained through a CMRP (command master religious program). Ultimately it is the commander, not the chaplain, who is accountable for his or her unit's religious program. In Iraq, I did not have a commander. I worked for Ambassador Bremer, a civilian. The religious support program in Baghdad was more or less my program rather than a command master religious support driven program.

1LT Carr and Carole Basri were instrumental in assisting me in accomplishing my goal for the free exercise of religion for all people in the CPA. By the time I departed Baghdad in May of 2004, weekly Jewish services were being held. They had also grown to the extent that each Friday at Shabbat there was a minion (ten men).

Chapter 14

Major General Paul Eaton

U.S. Army

The Battle of Karbala was fought on 10 October 680 on the Gregorian Calendar. The battle was fought between Huseyn ibn Ali, with an army of seventy-two, against the forces of Yazid I under the leadership of Umar ibn Sa'ad. Umar ibn Sa'ad's army consisted of forty thousand. It is self-evident that the army of Huseyn ibn Ali was easily defeated. It is reported that he, his family, and his army (totaling about 123 men, women, and children) were killed.

The Battle of Karbala is significant for a number of reasons. It is the defining event in the division between Sunni and Shia Muslims. The descendents of Huseyn ibn Ali are Shia. The descendents of Yazid I are the Sunni. The Battle of Karbala from the perspective of Shia Muslims was a glorious victory in that Huseyn Ali died in an attempt to reinstate the true values of Islam.

Yearly Shia pilgrims travel to Karbala, about fifty miles south of Baghdad, to celebrate the historic battle. Many faithful pilgrims will flagellate themselves in order to "share" the sufferings of Huseyn ibn Ali, his family, and the destruction of his army. The geopolitical significance of the Battle Karbala is that today Iraq and Iran are two of only five Muslim countries with a Shia majority. In Iraq, the Shia constitute 65 percent of the population. The Sunni constituency in Iraq amounts to about 32 percent of the population.

Hindsight is 20/20, or so it is claimed. One of the first policy decisions made by the Provisional Authority in Iraq was to disband the Iraqi army. There were many compelling reasons for its dissolution. The Iraqi army, especially the Republican Guard, had been Saddam's instrument for the repression of his people. It would be hard for the Coalition to assert that it was attempting to establish democracy in Iraq while continuing to use Saddam's forces to keep law and order. Saddam and the leadership of the Iraqi army were predominately Sunni. They had managed to keep the Shia majority and the Kurdish faction of northern Iraq in check through the vicious use of the Iraqi army. The Iraqi army was the regime's tool for the repression of its people, and the senior leadership of the Iraqi army was culpable in the genocide of the Kurds and Shia. Within the army itself, there was corruption and the maltreatment of its own soldiers. I met one former Iraqi soldier who had been imprisoned by the Iranians for ten years as a result of being captured during the Iran–Iraq War. He was released, returned to Iraq, and pressed into military service again just prior to Desert Storm. When he requested to visit his family after ten years as a captive in Iran, he was informed that he'd be shot for treason. He was to report to his new unit immediately! There was absolutely no way that the Coalition Provisional Authority could permit the Iraqi army to remain intact. Doing so would continue the Sunni domination of the Shia. It would only serve to perpetuate the division between Shia and Sunni begun at the Battle of Karbala.

In hindsight, there are many analysts who claim that it was a mistake to disband the Iraqi army following the invasion of Iraq. They claim that the Iraqi army could have been used to stabilize the country. This, in turn, would have mitigated the destruction and violence that has occurred in Iraq since 2003. I believe that this thinking is faulty for the reasons listed above. Saddam's Iraqi army was a corrupt organization led by criminals who terrorized their own people. It could never have been used as an instrument of democratization and stability. It is certainly true that disbanding the Iraqi army created a cadre of skilled individuals who could easily be assimilated by groups fighting against Coalition forces. I would argue, however, that the use of the Iraqi army to keep order following the invasion would have jeopardized the credibility of the United States and the Coalition Provisional Authority. How does the saying go? The definition of insanity is continuing to do the same thing while expecting different results.

Major General (MG) Paul Eaton was the CMATT (Coalition Military Assistance Training Team) commander. It was his responsibility and that of CMATT to build the new Iraqi army. In order to accomplish this mission, CMATT had to recruit, train, and field soldiers who were capable of defending their country. This was an enormous task and responsibility. How does one find recruits who place service to country above religious sectarianism? How does one find and train officers who are capable of leading soldiers? How does one vet those who want to serve in the new Iraqi army to make certain that they were not involved in crimes against the Iraqi people during Saddam's regime?

The CMATT offices were located at the north end of Saddam's former presidential palace in the ballroom. The ballroom had been added to the palace following the reconstruction effort after Desert Storm. It was a space somewhat larger than a soccer field. It was three or four stories high, with a vaulted ceiling and statuary at the base of the vaults where the ribs joined. Grand balconies on the second floor overlooked the ballroom, which was finished in marble. The palace was such a grand space with such grand areas that it was unusable for office space the way it was. Crews of construction workers were constantly dividing and subdividing the palace with plywood walls and partitions. Cables for electricity and communications crisscrossed floors and ceilings. More and bigger generators were continually in demand to provide the electricity necessary to keep up with the growth of the CPA. Blown fuses and blackouts were commonplace.

I have been informed that maintaining order and stability in a country requires twenty-five people per thousand. Those twenty-five people are soldiers, police officers, and others who maintain law. If this is an accurate accounting, then the reason for the chaos in Iraq following the invasion becomes abundantly clear. Iraq is a country of twenty-five million individuals and twelve and a half million AK-47 assault rifles! The Coalition undertook the invasion of Iraq with far fewer soldiers than were required—not to win the war, but to win the peace.

I am not privy to the inner workings of the Pentagon and the decisions that went into the planning estimates for the invasion of Iraq. It does appear to be widely known that General Shinseki's planning and estimates for the invasion and stability operations following the invasion required three hundred thousand troops. The invasion and stability operations were undertaken with about half that number. I believe that General Shinseki's estimates were probably based upon the lessons learned from the U.S. peacekeeping mission in Bosnia.

The dissolution of the Iraqi Army was not, in my opinion, the cause for destabilization in Iraq. The cause for the destabilization in Iraq following combat operations was the inability of the Coalition to adequately field the personnel required to maintain order within a country. Building an army and a police force from the ground up is a process that requires time.

I received a phone call from one of the ambassador's staff assistants. Would I go visit a Christian family that was living in one of the hooches behind the palace? The family consisted of a mother, her children, and her mother. The woman's husband had been murdered years earlier. He had been killed by some of Saddam's police. The woman knew the police official who was responsible for her husband's death. Moreover, she discovered that this same person had been vetted through the CPA process and was once again a police officer in the new Iraqi police force. She did not believe that she was safe and had passed this information on to CPA authorities. Ambassador Bremer had taken a personal interest in the welfare of this woman and her family. I believe that she became a CPA poster child of sorts and represented everything that the CPA was attempting to accomplish in Iraq. She had been brought into the Green Zone and given safe haven inside the palace compound. Her children played with the soldiers and civilians. They ate in the palace dining facility.

I prayed with this woman and her family on a number of occasions and visited them from time to time. The plan was that they were to be relocated to the United States and be given the opportunity to begin a new life. The date and time of their departure was kept confidential for security purposes. Even they didn't know when they were leaving Iraq. I do remember, however, that during one of my visits with the family a member of the ambassador's staff arrived and told them to get their things together because they were leaving.

The Iraqi police officer was removed from the police force. I am certain that he was charged in the death of the husband. Building a country is not an overnight endeavor. It takes time. It takes time to weed out the bad apples. It is easy for some people to slip through the cracks and perpetuate the past.

I did not work for MG Eaton, but he did call on me from time to time to assist in the development of CMATT and the new Iraqi army. The CMATT mission expanded exponentially when the United States determined to give the governing of Iraq back to the Iraqis. MG Eaton's mission suddenly jumped from creating nine battalions (the first Iraqi battalion had 700 personnel) for the new Iraqi army in two years to creating twenty-seven battalions in one year! I must say that MG Eaton did a singularly outstanding job as the CMATT Commander. He created an entirely new army from scratch while his mission kept expanding. His job was akin to that of trying to build an airplane while flying it. During the CMATT staffing process, I provided input for U.S. military chaplain and chaplain assistants to support their revised TO&E (table of organization and equipment).

MG Eaton was also intent upon making certain that soldiers in the new Iraqi army were provided with religious support. To that end we began to explore the possibility of a chaplaincy in the new Iraqi army. We also began vetting sheikhs (Muslim religious leaders) who would be willing to travel to Kirkush Military Training Base (KMTB) weekly to lead Muslim prayers on Fridays. This was a complex logistical issue, since the sheikhs all conducted services in Baghdad on Fridays. The original intention was to helicopter the sheikhs to KMTB, but that was not found to be a reliable source of travel because of other mission requirements.

I received another request from CMATT to visit Kirkush Military Training Base on 15 December 2003 to assist them in a very unique mission. Kirkush Military Training Base is not far from the border with Iran. The mountains of Iran are visible from the base on a clear day. I was to meet with representatives of the Yezidi sect.

> The Yezidi revere the Prophet Mohammed and the Sufi mystic Adi Musafir. . . . Adi is credited with writing many of the Yezidi Holy texts and is most likely to be the originator of the faith. Islamic writings mention the religion as early as the fourteenth century, but some scholars link them to Mithraism, Zoroastrianism, and even ancient Iraqi Buzzard worshippers.
>
> Yezidism is an enigma that has confounded scholars and incited debate for some time. The influence of Islam on the religion is heavy and obscures other aspects. Tantalizing clues point in every direction—rituals involving fire and prayers recited in the direction of the sun are distinctly Zoroastrian; taboos against eating lettuce and beans, baptisms, and the belief that Christ is a prophet hint at Manichaeism. Other unusual aspects of Yezidi belief are the reverence of an immortal elemental spirit named Khidir.[1]

Iraqi Muslims believe that Yezidis worship the devil. This is not the case, however, according to the Yezidis with whom I met. They believe that the devil has power, so they "give him his due."

The Yezidis who were being trained as part of the new Iraqi army at Kirkush Military Training Base were not being permitted to celebrate their own religious festivals. They were being forced to take block leave with the Muslim soldiers during the occasion of Muslim festivals. My mission was to meet with the Yezidi leaders in the new Iraqi army and learn from them the significant religious festivals in their religion. The information I received could then be taken into consideration during the planning process for future leave for Iraqi soldiers.

I found the Yezidi leaders to be very engaging, with a strong desire to please. They also made it a point to inform me that they did not worship the devil. I believe that they are extremely defensive about the accusation that they are devil worshippers. My impression was that the Yezidis are a people who have lived in a part of the world that has been conquered by armies throughout history. Little by little they assimilated portions of the religions of the peoples that conquered them. When I departed Kirkush Military Training Base, I had learned about six important religious festivals in the Yezidi religion.

✢

One issue that has been hotly debated in the United States is our strategy for the removal of U.S. forces from Iraq. I believe that the answer to that question is really rather simple. The implementation of the strategy, however, is extremely complex. Coalition forces, to include U.S. troops, can leave Iraq when the Iraqis have enough of a stability force to maintain law and order within their country. That doesn't just mean recruiting and training twenty-five people per thousand (or whatever the formula is for stability); it means creating leaders who can manage the forces. It means creating command and control systems within the police force and army. It means establishing a force with ethical principals that transcend religious and regional differences. The withdrawal of all U.S. forces from Iraq is really quite simple. It is just not an easy task that can be implemented in the blink of an eye.

✢

Following Operation Desert Storm, the United States encouraged the Kurds in northern Iraq to rise up against Saddam Hussein. They did. We did not, however, support them to the extent that they could be successful. We did establish the Iraqi northern no-fly zone to prevent Saddam from interdicting them from the air. That was about the extent of our support. Thousands were killed in reprisal.

The United States has encouraged the Iraqi people to embrace freedom and establish a democratic government. We invaded Iraq and enlisted the aid of thousands of Iraqis. The question about whether or not we should have gone to war in the first place is moot. We did go to war. We removed the Baathist Party from power and disbanded Saddam's Iraqi Army. The pragmatic question that we must now debate is when do we withdraw our forces and economic assistance from Iraq? Do we do it immediately or do we remain in Iraq until stability is established and until such time was the Iraqis can maintain their own security? I do not believe that the United States has a responsibility to remain in Iraq until the thirteen-hundred-year-old conflict between the Shia and Sunni is ameliorated. On the other hand, I do not believe that we can simply declare victory and leave. I would prefer to see a carefully considered exit strategy for U.S. forces in Iraq. Furthermore, it would be my earnest desire that our exit strategy be based upon our moral and ethical obligations toward those Iraqis who have risked everything to work with us rather than the self-serving expediency of aspiring politicians.

I was interested in listening to American soldiers talk about their experiences working with the new Iraqi army in 2007 while stationed in Kuwait. What they told me was startling. They said that they preferred to conduct operations in the cities with Iraqi soldiers rather than on their own. They told me that when they were on their own they became targets of sniper fire and IEDs. When they were on patrol with soldiers from the new Iraqi army, however, they were safe. It appeared to them that the new Iraqi army is becoming accepted and respected by the Iraqi people.

Chapter 15

The Grandson of the Ayatollah Khomeini

The Arabic word *iftar* means breakfast (fast-breaking). Iftar is also the meal that ends the daily fast for faithful Muslims during Ramadan. Fasting is one of the five pillars of the Muslim religion and includes both food and drink. Muslims also refrain from smoking and sexual relations during their Ramadan fast. Fasting during Ramadan begins prior to sunup and ends following sundown. Iftar is not only a meal; it is more of a celebration. One can well imagine that having a cold drink following a scorching day in the desert is cause for celebration.

Chaplains in the U.S. Army brief their commanders prior to Ramadan that soldiers traveling outside of forward operating bases respect the Muslim fast by not eating or drinking in public view. Commanders are reminded that Muslim contractors working with the military are not to be improperly employed during Ramadan. In other words, do not have them working out in the sun all day long when they are inhibited from drinking. There are a number of other things of which U.S. military personnel need to be aware when operating in predominately Muslim countries.

Prior to Ramadan during my year in Iraq, I made certain that Muslim personnel assigned to or working in support of the Coalition Provision Authority were able to eat in the dining facility before sunup and after sundown. The dining facility had standard hours of operation, and my insistence that we accommodate Muslims would mean a change in our contract with the company operating it. The minor adjustment of dining facility hours of operations required integrated planning well in advance. Not only did the contractor have to adjust work schedules, but also the CPA had to publish the changes made to the hours of operation. It would be useless to adjust the hours of operation if Muslims couldn't take advantage of the provision.

I was invited to present a workshop at the annual conference of the Consortium of Endowed Episcopal Parishes in the year following my deployment to Iraq. The keynote speaker at the conference was Ms. Madeleine Albright, the Secretary of State in the Clinton Administration. I was particularly interested in hearing what she had to say because I felt personally embarrassed by her in my interaction with Mr. Mustafa Terzic in Tuzla, Bosnia, in 1998.

One of my responsibilities at Eagle Base, Bosnia, had been coordinating U.S. military assistance in the establishment of the Tuzla International Airport colocated at the airfield on Eagle Base. The Bosnian heading up the project was Mr. Mustafa Terzic. He was a very capable planner and administrator who had the political savvy to succeed in this project. In other words, he was a former Communist bureaucrat. But he was an outgoing, likable guy who was extremely intelligent. It was my responsibility to act as his liaison to the U.S. military.

The day was finally approaching for the grand opening of the airport. Everything had been set, guests had been invited, an airline would begin service, and dignitaries from throughout Bosnia would be present. This was truly a big deal because it highlighted the renewal of Bosnia following the war.

A couple of days prior to the opening of the airport, I was instructed to inform Mr. Terzic that the grand opening of the Tuzla International Airport was being postponed. I was not permitted to tell him the reason for this postponement, however. It was made clear to me that Madeleine Albright had learned of the event and had nixed the opening date herself. The reason was really quite simple: Bosnia was just about to hold "free and open" elections. The United States had a vested interest in who won these "free and open" elections, and the individuals running for election who would benefit most by the publicity gained through the opening of the Tuzla International Airport were not the people we wanted elected! Therefore, I was to inform Mr. Terzic that the date had been postponed.

That was one of my most embarrassing moments as an America citizen. I felt ashamed of what I'd become a party to. Bosnia was to have "free and open" elections that our Secretary of State was attempting to manipulate. When the election results were received, the postponement of the grand opening of the Tuzla International Airport proved to have no impact. The people whom the U.S. didn't want elected got elected anyhow.

The important point that I took away from Ms. Albright's keynote address was that the State Department needed to become more focused on religious engagement. That's what I took to be the gist of what she said, and I heartily agree with her. She also suggested that had she to do it over again, she would place more emphasis on religion and its role in international relations. Again, I am in full agreement with her. It is most unfortunate, however, that she learned this lesson after her tenure as Secretary of State.

✝

One of my mantras as the Chaplain for the Coalition Provisional Authority was "religion drives the train in Iraq." In the absence of political stability, it is the religious leaders in Iraq, along with the tribal leaders, who possess the power to establish and maintain peace.

I believe that our engagement at the ambassadorial level in international engagement is blind to the necessity for religious engagement. As Americans, we wear blinders that have grown out of the "separation of church and state." Because we live in a culture that emphasizes the disassociation of religion and government, we take this cultural baggage with us wherever we go. Our blinders prevent us from striving for a religious resolution to world issues as well as a political solution.

The Coalition Provisional Authority was an organization established to govern Iraq until such time as the Iraqi people established their own government. When the interim Iraqi government was prepared to govern, the CPA would disappear. The United States would then establish an embassy in Baghdad to interface with the new Iraqi leadership. The U.S. embassy would retain the use of Saddam's former presidential palace until a new embassy was constructed.

The transition from the Coalition Provisional Authority to the U.S. Embassy required careful and long-range planning. A team from the State Department came to Baghdad months in advance for coordination purposes and weekly meetings were held to discuss every aspect of the transition. During our first meeting, all of the section directors briefed the State Department advance team on their mission and significant issues regarding transition. Following my brief, the team chief looked over at me and said that he didn't understand why I was even present. He made it clear that the State Department doesn't have chaplains or chapels and that there was nothing I had to say that was of importance to them! I took his remarks not as personally insulting but as a further indication of the myopic view our State Department exhibits when it comes to religious engagement.

The truth of the matter is that the U.S. Embassy that is now situated at Saddam's former presidential palace does have a chapel. The chapel is no longer situated inside the palace. A separate building has been constructed on the grounds in front of the southern wing of the palace. Even State Department employees working in a combat zone and having their friends and coworkers killed indiscriminately discover the need for religious support.

CH (COL) Doug Carver, now Major General Carver and Chief of Army Chaplains approached me one afternoon and asked if I would be interested in sharing Iftar with the grandson of the Ayatollah Khomeini. CH Carver served as the command chaplain for the 5th Corps and also for CJTF-7 (Combined Joint Task Force 7). He had an office in the presidential palace on the second floor, but his primary base of operations was Camp Victory, about ten miles away. He expressed some concern about traveling in Baghdad at night and wanted to know what I thought about the idea. I jumped at the opportunity and stated that I thought we'd be fine with two vehicles and our chaplain assistants for security. U.S. military chaplains are noncombatants and do not carry weapons. I generally put it this way: "We may only be shot at; we can't return fire." To provide security on the battlefield, chaplains and chaplain assistants work as a unit ministry team. Chaplain assistants are responsible for keeping their chaplains alive. It is they who carry weapons. I have always preferred chaplain assistants that are good soldiers. If I was forced to choose between a "highly religious chaplain wannabe" assistant and a "crusty NCO with an attitude who can shoot" assistant, I'd take the crusty NCO every time.

CH Carver and I decided that we would attend Iftar with the grandson of the Ayatollah Khomeini. The invitation was set for 11 November at a private home in the city.

Saddam, during one of his purges, drained the marshlands of southern Iraq and displaced the marsh people, whom he saw as a threat. I am certain that the destruction of a culture and way of life also accompanied the draining of the marshes. I was about to get a glimpse into the culture of the marsh people in a most unusal way.

CH Carver and I, along with three or four chaplain assistants, found our way to the Baghdad home where we were to share Iftar with the ayatollah's grandson. A ten- or twelve-foot-high wall surrounded the home, and armed guards manned the entrance. Behind the house a reed hut had been constructed in the style of the marsh people. The hut was about fourteen feet wide, thirty or more feet long, and twelve feet high. Supporting columns made of bundled reeds were four feet in diameter at the base and got progressively narrower toward the top of the structure. Reeds woven together served as the walls. Had one turned the structure over, it would have looked like the hull of a boat. Rugs covered the ground, and shoes (boots) were removed before one entered. Just inside the entrance to the hut was a brazier for boiling water to be used for preparing Arab coffee. The hut had been outfitted with electricity. There were lights and paddle fans hanging from the ceiling, and portable air conditioning units had been installed. There were also electrical outlets near the base of the structure. It was a magnificent building that had been constructed in only six days.

We were led into the hut and introduced to the grandson of the ayatollah and the others who were present. I think there may have been as many as twenty of us all together. We sat along the sides of the hut, resting against large pillows. The linguist was an American woman in her mid to late twenties. I was shocked that a woman was to serve as our linguist and also have dinner with us. I noticed, however, that she was extremely astute in the role she assumed within the group. She took a submissive posture in both her mannerism and in her speaking. It appeared to work very well with these Arab men and also with the grandson of the ayatollah, who is not an Arab. Iranians are not Arabs, they are Persians.

The grandson of the ayatollah is a charismatic figure. He is a Sufi Muslim. The Sufis are Muslim mystics. I knew something about Sufism and was intrigued to be speaking with him. I was also astounded by what he had to say. The grandson of the Ayatollah Khomeini believes that the United States is the one country that should serve as a blueprint for the rest of the world. He stated that people who live in the United States have different racial, cultural, religious, and political backgrounds but all manage to live together in relatively harmony. As I listed to him, I imagined that his grandfather must have been spinning in his grave!

I was also interested in hearing his religious views. The more he spoke, the more I felt as if he were my brother on the same spiritual path. I felt more akin to him in many ways than I do with some Christian clergy I meet. Here was a holy man who had deep insights into one's relationship with God and the application of that to one's relationship with fellow human beings. I would have loved to spend days with him asking questions and comparing ideas.

Dinner was brought into the hut on large trays, and we all helped ourselves to this common meal. Following dinner, dessert plates were brought to us with typical eastern treats containing finely chopped nuts and honey in layers of philo dough. The fellow tending the brazier brought coffee to us in small demitasse cups. Cigars were given to all of us following dessert, and we reclined against the pillows in the hut and chatted for quite a while. At one point, a telephone rang; someone answered it and handed it to the grandson of the ayatollah. He then handed it to me. I was a bit taken back that someone would be calling me through him. It turned out to be an Arab cleric who had approached me about a religious institute he wanted to establish in Iraq working for peace and reconciliation. He wanted the CPA to give him three million dollars over a multiyear period. I began to wonder if I'd been invited to share Iftar with the grandson of the ayatollah in order that some Iraqi religious leaders could elicit my assistance in the project. CH Carver was keen on the idea and encouraged my support both prior to and after the Iftar.

We returned to the Green Zone about 2100 hours and parked our vehicles in the lot across the street from the palace. I believe that I returned to my office, and I believe that CH Carver and the CJTF-7 chaplain assistants returned to Camp Victory. Twenty minutes later a huge explosion rocked the palace. A twenty-foot long Russian-made rocket exploded in the parking lot we had just vacated. Six vehicles were completely demolished, and fourteen others were damaged. Shrapnel cut through the SUVs like a knife through butter. The difference between life and death that evening had been just twenty minutes. Were it not for CH Carver, we would have visited with the grandson of the Ayatollah Khomeini a bit longer that evening. He didn't want us to be out on the streets of Baghdad too late, however. His decision to leave may very well have saved all our lives.

I can't help but wonder what effect might be achieved if our State Department were able to remove its cultural blinders and leverage the good will of religious leaders to achieve peace and stability in the war-torn regions of the world.

I wonder what it would be like if we stopped talking about all the wars that have taken place in the name of Allah and began to consider all the violence that has been prevented in the name of Allah. Military commanders involved in decision making don't want to hear what individual members of their staffs think about particular courses of action. They want to be given facts, and they base their decisions upon the facts they receive. It is time to stop listening to those who love to blame religion for the ills of humanity as if they actually know what they were talking about or were basing their opinions on factual evidence. Fact: the major conflicts of the twentieth century were not religiously motivated. World War I, World War II, the Korean War, the Vietnam War (for the United States), the Afghan War (for the U.S.S.R.), and the Cold War were not fought because of religion.

I dare say that religion has contributed far more to the quest for human dignity in world history than to the perpetuation of conflict. It is not religion that has precipitated the greatest loss of life in our time and that of our parents and grandparents, but the lack thereof.

The religious leaders of Iraq, in the absence of civil authority, have the ability to influence their people. The U.S. cultural blinders of the separation between church and state inhibit us from engaging them and also from achieving our desired end state.

Chapter 16

Saddam Hussein

During the invasion of Iraq U.S. military personnel were issued decks of playing cards. The faces of these playing cards identified the "most wanted" Iraqi leaders that the United States was interested in capturing. Saddam Hussein was pictured on the ace of spades, and his sons Uday and Qusay were the ace of hearts and the ace of clubs, respectively. I believe that the idea behind the playing cards was that troops would become familiar with the most wanted Iraqi leaders by playing cards with their buddies. They would then be able to identify them on sight. I am not exactly certain when the personnel to whom the decks of cards were distributed had the time to play cards. Troops preparing for and conducting combat operations don't have time to do much of anything except prepare themselves for battle. During my entire year in Iraq, I never had the time to play cards, nor did any of my friends. Nevertheless, the decks of cards did make a great souvenir and Christmas stocking-stuffer for the folks back home.

The idea of using cards to teach military personnel was nothing new. During the Cold War soldiers were given decks of cards with friendly and enemy vehicles, armor, and planes. We were expected to study these cards so we would know what or what not to engage. The Army used every device imaginable to educate its soldiers. I had served in a combat engineer battalion and would visit the motor pool occasionally to check in with the soldiers working there. Updates to repair manuals and new procedures for repairing vehicles were not distributed to soldiers in long, dry, and boring FMs (field manuals). Soldiers working in the motor pool received updates by way of comic books. I guess that someone figured out that soldiers would actually read comic books. FMs were updated as necessary, but the primary tool for keeping mechanics informed was comic books.

✢

The capture of Saddam, Uday, and Qusay was so important to the United States that a bounty was placed upon their heads. A $15 million reward was offered for the capture of Uday or Qusay, and Saddam's capture was worth

$25 million. I know that U.S. military personnel were not entitled to receive a reward for capturing Saddam or his sons, but that did not stop me from checking my closets at the Al-Rasheed Hotel every evening after work. I'd slide open the closet door across from the bathroom and exclaim, "Saddam are you hiding in here? I certainly hope so, because I could use the money!" When I'd go into the rooms of some of my civilian contractor friends, I always asked them if they'd checked their closets that day for Saddam so that they could receive the $25 million reward. It always brought a laugh and a thorough examination of their closets.

Uday and Qusay were both killed by U.S. forces on 22 July 2003. Saddam was captured 13 December 2003 by soldiers of the 4th ID (infantry division). On both these occasions there was great rejoicing by the Iraqi people. The day workers at the palace chanted or sang as they were lined up at the end of the day for roll call prior to departing. Gunfire could be heard throughout the city. Of course, gunfire was always heard throughout the city. This occurred so frequently that one didn't take too much notice of it after a while.

It was disconcerting, however, for those who had just been assigned to the Coalition Provisional Authority. I remember our daily run one afternoon with a new addition to our group. He was wide-eyed with fright as he heard rifle fire just across the Tigris River from us as we ran down a road adjacent to the water. Bombed-out buildings, explosions, and gun shots were so commonplace, however, that one ceased to notice them at all after a short time.

On the day of Saddam's capture and on the day that Uday and Qusay were killed, one knew that the gunfire was not directed at U.S. forces. It was celebratory fire. What's the old adage? What goes up must come down. Celebratory fire is just as dangerous as fire directed at someone. On more than one occasion, someone at the CPA would report that he or she returned to his or her hooch only to find a small hole in the roof of the connex and a bullet lying on the bed or floor. Individuals were wounded and killed from time to time by celebratory fire.

When I visit someone's home, I find that I learn a lot about that person. It is as if their home speaks to me. It communicates to me everything I need to know about that person. I can tell within a few moments if I'll be comfortable with them or not. I get to know them, not just by their possessions but also by the manner in which their furniture is arranged and the home is decorated. I lived in Saddam's former presidential palace for six or eight weeks and then worked at the palace for a year. I got to know Saddam through his palace. I became acquainted with him day in and day out by observing him through his possessions. Let me take us on a tour through the palace and see what we come to find out about Saddam.

The front façade of the palace had three grand entrances. There was the center entrance and portico leading into the rotunda. There was the north portico and entrance leading into a grand foyer. The south end of the palace had a portico matching the one for the northern foyer except that the motif was entirely different from that of the northern entrance. My office and the first of three chapels I was given for the conduct of religious support were located in the southern end of the palace. If I entered the palace in front, I always entered from the south.

The grand foyer was beautifully adorned in a Chaldean style. The colors were rich maroon and gold. Ornate balconies looked down from the second floor twenty or thirty feet above. The walls, ceiling, and floor were all clad in marble. Entry into this space was granted through twelve- or fourteen-foot-high wooden doors decorated in bronze. Throughout the south entrance Saddam's monogram had been incorporated into the decorative marble. Saddam surrounded everyone who entered the palace via the southern entrance.

A short hallway connected the southern entrance to the main hallway running along the north-south axis of the building. There was a large marble triptych on the southern wall of the short hallway. I was intrigued by this sculpture and began studying it each time I entered or exited the palace through the south portico. The right panel of the triptych showed something being handed from one individual to another. The theme of this section was the presentation of the law to Hammurabi by the deity Shamash. The Hammurabic Code was certainly an "eye for an eye" judicial system, with capital punishment the sentence for a whole host of criminal acts.

1. If any one ensnare another, putting a ban upon him, but he can not prove it, then he that ensnared him shall be put to death.
8. If any one steal cattle or sheep, or an ass, or a pig or a goat, if it belong to a god or to the court, the thief shall pay thirtyfold therefor; if they belonged to a freed man of the king he shall pay tenfold; if the thief has nothing with which to pay he shall be put to death.
15. If any one take a male or female slave of the court, or a male or female slave of a freed man, outside the city gates, he shall be put to death.
22. If any one is committing a robbery and is caught, then he shall be put to death.

> 25. If fire break out in a house, and some one who comes to put it out cast his eye upon the property of the owner of the house, and take the property of the master of the house, he shall be thrown into that self-same fire.[1]

The marble triptych was not far from the "intimidation room" that had been given to me for use as a chapel. The intimidation room was so named because individuals would be called into the room and required to stand before Saddam to learn their fates. One was as likely to be sentenced to death as not when being summoned by Saddam. One entered the intimidation room by one of seven sets of doors and then had to walk quite some distance to reach Saddam's throne. Surrounding the room would be seated various dignitaries of the Baathist regime. Saddam's law was not a code like the one given Hammurabi by Shamash, but his personal whim on any particular day.

The center panel on the triptych depicted two hands cupped with a waterfall flowing from them. It also depicted wheat springing from the ground beneath. I never really understood the meaning of this section of the sculpture until I introduced it to one of the art historians working with the CPA in the restoration and preservation of Iraqi antiquities. He explained to me that the waterfall and the wheat symbolize prosperity.

Many soldiers who were deployed to Saudi Arabia during Desert Storm got the bright idea to buy Iraqi dinars for investment purposes. I too bought quite a few twenty dinar notes in Saudi banks. It seemed like a good idea at the time because the Iraqi dinar had been worth three U.S. dollars, and the expectation was that it would once again increase in value. When I was in Baghdad in 2003, the U.S. dollar was worth 14,000 Iraqi dinars. The regime of Saddam Hussein was not a time of great prosperity for the Iraqi people. He devalued the currency of the nation and almost bankrupted the country by his war with Iran and then his subsequent invasion of Kuwait. During his years in power the country experienced economic hardship. The Iraqi dinars I purchased in Saudi Arabia are worthless today. Over the years I had them framed and gave them as unique gifts to friends. The soldiers who made a killing by purchasing foreign currency in Saudi Arabia did so by purchasing Kuwaiti dinars.

The left-hand panel in the triptych is the depiction of war horses pulling chariots and with battle flags flying. The background scene in this section of the sculpture is the very top of the Dome of the Rock in Jerusalem. I am convinced that Saddam Hussein saw himself as the new Nebuchadnezzar. It was Nebuchadnezzar who had conquered Jerusalem and deported the Jews into captivity in Babylon. Saddam was to be the new Nebuchadnezzar, who would conquer Jerusalem and place the Jews in captivity once again. Saddam was fascinated by the history of Babylon and was a King Nebuchadnezzar wannabe.

The triptych panels summarized who Saddam saw himself to be. He was the recipient of the law handed down to him from Shamash through Hammurabi. He was the giver of prosperity. And he was the new Nebuchadnezzar. There was one more symbol of note in the sculpture. At the top of the triptych in the center was a stylized carving of the sun. Its light made law and prosperity and world conquest possible. In the center of the sun was the monogram for Saddam Hussein.

The center entrance to the palace led up a flight of stairs and into the rotunda. Before one entered the rotunda, however, one saw an inscription had been affixed to the marble wall. It was made of gold-colored Arabic letters attached to stanchions protruding about six inches from the wall. The inscription was a tribute to Saddam and his victory in the First Gulf War! Saddam had turned the utter collapse and defeat of his army in four days into a glorious victory over the coalition forces. One walked into the rotunda to find a huge portrait of Saddam hanging above the first story on the back wall. Saddam was portrayed handing a brick to a worker during the rebuilding process.

The United States knew that it wanted to use the palace following Operation Iraqi Freedom as headquarters for the rebuilding and restoration of Iraq. For this reason it was not targeted during the air campaign prior to the ground invasion. We did manage to hit most of the other governmental buildings surrounding the palace, including Uday's compound across the street from the presidential palace. What military planners failed to comprehend, however, is that the chillers for the palace air conditioning system were located in Uday's compound. We totally obliterated that facility and suffered without air conditioning well into the summer months.

Saddam probably had little, if anything, to do with the physical reconstruction of the presidential palace, but one would never guess that from the painting in the rotunda. The center entrance to the palace portrays Saddam as the victorious leader of Iraq who rebuilt his nation after Desert Storm.

The northern entrance to the palace, which eventually became the chapel during my tenure in Iraq, was similar in style to the southern foyer but differently appointed. It had light-colored marble walls and floor. The ceiling was the most prominent feature of the entrance area. It was many stories high and unlike any architecture I'd ever seen before. I can best describe it as the inside shell of a three-sided pyramid. The "stones" of the pyramid were set progressively up and in toward the center of the foyer. The ninety-nine names of Allah as recorded in the Qur'an decorated the "stones" or blocks that formed the pyramid. A great chandelier hung from the center of the ceiling.

One of the things I learned about Saddam Hussein from the Iraqis who visited the palace is that he had attributed to himself ninety-nine names. It was evident that he was not to be outdone by Allah and fancied himself as possessing the same power and authority as God. During one occasion with party officials, someone mentioned that Saddam was not like God because while he could take life, only God could give life. Immediately Saddam sent for some unsuspecting palace worker. The fellow was brought before Saddam and on the spot was sentenced to death. The poor fellow had done absolutely nothing wrong to deserve the punishment of death. Everyone present was dumbfounded by this act. Then Saddam turned to the fellow who he had just sentenced to death and the others present and said to the fellow, "I pardon you." Then he turned to those who were present and informed them that he too had the power to give life because he had just given life back to the fellow who was sentenced to die.

Iraqi women cover their heads when they go out. Of course, all Muslim women cover themselves, but in Iraq during the reign of Saddam Hussein it was for a different reason. One Iraqi woman working at the palace informed me that the women in Iraq feared going out in public looking attractive. They preferred looking dowdy on the street. The reason for this was that they could easily be picked up, raped, and murdered. For as notorious a leader as he was, Saddam couldn't hold a candle to his son Uday. Uday raped and murdered many women whom he found desirable. His actions gave carte blanche to other thugs within the government to do the same.

Living in the former presidential palace in Iraq I got to know Saddam Hussein. I learned how he saw himself, as depicted in the art and decoration of the palace. Saddam perceived of himself as the sun that shone down on Iraq to bring law and prosperity to the Iraqi people. He believed that he was the new Nebuchadnezzar who would once again conquer Jerusalem (Israel) and return the Jewish people to captivity. He fancied himself as a great victorious leader who had defeated the coalition forces during Operation Desert Storm. And he saw himself as having as many attributes as God and having the power to both take and give life.

The reality of Saddam Hussein as revealed in the poverty of his country and the manner in which he terrorized his people is quite different. He wasn't a lawgiver bringing order to Iraq. Instead, he brought fear and death to the land. He wasn't a waterfall that brought prosperity to the land; he was a tyrant who brought financial ruin. He wasn't the new King Nebuchadnezzar who subdued the Jews and initiated another Babylonian Captivity. He wasn't a god who could give life. He was merely a thug who took the lives of thousands upon thousands of his people.

One thing that is said about human beings is that we demonize our enemies in order to justify going to war against them. In both Operation Desert Storm and Operation Iraqi Freedom, the United States and its coalition partners never had to demonize Saddam Hussein. He managed to do that all by himself without our assistance.

Chapter 17

Philip Bloom

The CAR (Chief of the Army Reserve) ordered a one-day stand-down for all reserve soldiers in response to the events at Abu Ghraib prison. The purpose of the stand-down was to listen to ethics briefings and to conduct small-group discussion in response to scenarios that posed ethical and moral challenges for leaders. Major General (MG) Dennis Laich, Commander of the 94th RRC (Regional Readiness Command), went a step further. He called me into his office months well in advance of the stand-down and informed me that I was to personally conduct ethics briefings for all of the 94th RRC subordinate units with a commander in the rank of LTC or above.

I had just received my commander's guidance from MG Laich, but I wanted one more thing from him. "Sir," I said, "if you could capture the essence of moral decision making in a few words, what would you say? When I brief your soldiers, I'd like to give them some simple guidelines that come straight from their commander."

MG Laich hesitated for a moment and said, "Chaplain let me think about that and get back to you."

The following day, my CG (commanding general) gave to me three simple tests as a way to assist soldiers evaluate whether or not they are standing on morally solid ground. First, "Would you take this action if your wife and children were watching you?" Second, "Would you be comfortable reading a factual account of what you had done on the front page of the *Boston Globe*?" Third, "Would you be secure in knowing that the person who witnessed what you had done is your worst enemy?" Is it any wonder that this man rose to the rank of Major General? His moral decision-making guidance for his command was simple, straightforward, easy to understand, and right on the mark.

✝

Chaplains in the U.S. Army have quite a few responsibilities. One of our responsibilities is to assist soldiers in not losing their moral compass in peacetime or in the midst of war. On the day that the Al-Rasheed Hotel was rocketed, all of us living there were moved to other locations. I was taken with a group of thirty people over to the "K" annex. The "K" annex was a newly renovated compound inside the Green Zone that was home to a signal company from the Iowa National Guard. The company commander, CPT (captain) Aaron Cooper, was a friend of mine who was active in chapel services and who also led a Christian men's group at 0630 hours every Wednesday in my office. I arrived at the "K" annex expecting to share a room with five other displaced individuals from the Al-Rasheed Hotel. Instead, CPT Cooper spotted me and informed me that I would be billeted with him. He and I were to share a private "efficiency apartment" consisting of a bedroom, bathroom, and shower area. I am actually making it sound much nicer than it was. The room in which CPT Cooper and I were living had not been renovated along with the other buildings in the annex. In the center of our bedroom ceiling there was a large iron or steel hook. It was not the only room I'd seen in the Green Zone that had such a device. I had the eerie feeling that this room had been used by Saddam's secret police and that the hook was at just the right height for hanging individuals from ropes tied around their wrists or upside down from ropes bound around their feet. The room that CPT Cooper and I shared also had no real protection in the event of a bomb blast. There were many evening when explosions could be heard throughout the Green Zone and the concussion felt inside our room. Should a rocket or mortar land adjacent to our "hooch," there was nothing to prevent it from demolishing our little building or sending glass shards flying toward us from the door and windows. On one evening of intense bombardment in Baghdad by our own forces, I secretly hoped that their aim was good. I certainly did not want to be in "K" annex if it was hit. The annex was my third residence in Baghdad, and I was to live there for about three months.

CPT Cooper was a very intelligent commander who just happened to be an Annapolis graduate. His favorite food in the world was Rice Crispy treats, which he "inhaled" with great delight. I don't know how he ended up in the Army rather than the Navy, but it was the Army's gain. During the months that we shared the hooch at the "K" annex, there were a number of occasions when CPT Cooper sought my advice regarding the moral conduct of his troops and how he might respond to errant or immoral behavior.

✢

I met Philip Bloom at the presidential palace in 2003. I am not exactly certain how we met. It is possible that he may have come to my office to speak to me, or we may have just bumped into each other in the dining facility or on the palace grounds. What I do remember about him is that he was an outgoing and engaging fellow sixty years of age. He was a Yeshiva University graduate who had been living and working in Romania for the past few years. He had gone into business there because the corporate climate was much more favorable in Romania than in the United States. He had come to Baghdad to offer his products and services to the Coalition Provisional Authority. I remember him showing me a catalog of containerized living compartments that his company could produce. They actually looked nicer than the connexes in which we were living. He wanted to compete for contracts being sent out for bid by the CPA. I studied the brochure he handed me and told him that I'd be happy to put him in contact with an individual who could tell him the contractual process for having his products considered. He told me that he'd be happy to pay me a finder's fee for assisting him. I remember thinking what a thoughtful gesture that was, but I assured him that the Army paid me quite well and I was more than happy to assist him for free, knowing that he was attempting to improve the quality of life for the personnel assigned to the CPA. I ran into Philip Bloom from time to time, and he dropped by my office on occasion to use my computer.

Going to war is an incredibly fantastic experience if one lives through it. The bonds and friendship that are developed during wartime unite individuals for life. It is difficult to pinpoint exactly why this is so. Perhaps it is that living constantly with the threat of death makes one interdependent with one's friends. Perhaps it is the shared experience of living together under stressful conditions. Whatever the case, I come away from my time in Iraq believing that the community I experience there is what the *ecclesia* (Greek term meaning the "gathering" or "community"—in Christianity it refers to the church) is intended to be. One year in Iraq revealed things about community that the church was not able to reveal to me in fifty-some years. I say this not as a criticism of the church but to highlight the incredible bond that is established by individuals who survive the horrors of war.

The survival of war, however, is not merely physical endurance. There are a great many individuals who return from war scarred for life, yet their bodies bear no mark or injury. Individuals may die in any number of ways in war. I had a soldier brought to me by our security officer who was suffering the "long night of the soul." This soldier had been on guard duty inside the Green Zone throughout the night. At 0400 hours, a car came speeding toward the checkpoint he was guarding traveling in the wrong direction. He signaled for the vehicle to stop. It did not. He then fired his rifle into the air, but the vehicle continued toward the checkpoint at high speed. He then aimed his weapon at the windshield of the vehicle and fired. The vehicle stopped immediately. The individual riding in the passenger seat had been killed. The soldier had acted promptly and in accordance with the ROE (rules of engagement). His quick action would most certainly have saved the lives of his fellow soldiers had the vehicle been a car bomb. Upon further investigation, however, it was discovered that the driver had no harmful intent. He was just a fellow in the wrong place at the wrong time driving too quickly in the wrong direction and ignoring the instructions from the sentry at the checkpoint.

The other guards at the checkpoint told this young man that he had done the correct thing. The officers in his chain of command reinforced the notion that he had acted appropriately and in accordance with the ROE. The only problem was that nothing said to him worked to allay the remorse and guilt he was feeling. He had just killed someone who intended him no harm and he could not forgive himself.

It was because of this that the CPA security officer brought him to see me. He was unfit for duty until such time as he could work through this tragic event. What if a car approached his checkpoint at a high rate of speed in the future and failed to respond to his warning? Would he hesitate to act? What if next time the vehicle was laden with a car bomb? Would he be the cause of an explosion that killed him and his buddies? The security officer wanted me to counsel him.

So, what does one say to a young soldier who has just taken the life of an innocent? There is nothing, absolutely nothing that anyone can say to make it all go away. There are no magic words or formulas that make everything right. All one can do is listen and perhaps begin the process of allowing another to come to grips with his guilt, remorse, and sin. Returning from war alive is not merely an issue of the body; it is an issue of the soul.

CPT Cooper had a soldier in his company who was more than troubled. This soldier was acting in such a bizarre fashion that he was sent to the 113th Combat Stress Detachment for a psychiatric evaluation. He was returned as fit for duty. His peculiar behavior continued, so CPT Cooper had his weapon removed from him. For a soldier to have a weapon removed from him in a combat theater is an extraordinary occurrence. Soldiers need their weapons for protection. CPT Cooper also had this soldier confined to his bedroom at night and another soldier assigned to keep watch outside his door.

The "K" annex was located in a neighborhood within the Green Zone. Iraqi families lived in the houses along the street on which the compound was situated. One day this soldier and one of his soldier buddies were out in the neighborhood. They found a kitten belonging to one of the neighborhood children and, in front of these children, the soldier took out a knife and proceeded to cut off the kitten's head and paws!

CPT Cooper sought me out and asked my advice. The first thing I suggested to him was that he needed to go have a chat with the family that owned the kitten as soon as possible. He told me later that he found the mother of these children sitting on her front stoop sobbing when he went to the house. She wanted to know why American soldiers hate pets.

I also suggested that the soldier who did this must be given another psychological evaluation, receive treatment for his sickness in the U.S., and be discharged from the Army. The U.S. Army cannot afford to have troops like this carrying weapons or making life-and-death decisions. We are certainly not going to win the local population over to our side by terrorizing their children and murdering their pets!

Philip Bloom did end up making contact with individuals who were in the position to hire him to provide products and services for the reconstruction of Iraq. Unfortunately, he became involved in a scheme to bilk the U.S. government out of millions of dollars. What was even more perplexing to me is that one of the individuals accused in this plan to defraud the U.S. government was an acquaintance of mine from my former Army unit.

According to federal prosecutors, LTC Debra Harrison returned home from Iraq with $80,000 more in income than the government paid her. She sent weapons home to her husband, who was also implicated in the scheme. And she had a Cadillac Escalade waiting for her at a local car dealership upon her return to the U.S. Deb Harrison and I deployed together with the 358th Civil Affairs Brigade in Bosnia. I was in Tuzla and she was stationed with our contingent in Sarajevo. Debra survived her tour in Bosnia but was not as fortunate in Iraq. In losing her moral compass, she also lost her life. LTC Harrison is awaiting trial in federal court for her participation in the Philip Bloom scheme.

Wikipedia has this to say about Philip Bloom:

> Philip Bloom is an American businessman who pled guilty on April 18, 2006 to conspiracy, bribery and money laundering in connection with a scheme to defraud the Coalition Provisional Authority–South Central Region (CPA-SC) during the occupation of Iraq. Bloom was accused of bribing Lieutenant Colonel Bruce D. Hopfengardner, Lieutenant Colonel Michael Wheeler,

> Lieutenant Colonel Debra Harrison and a CPA Comptroller and convicted felon named Robert Stein Jr. Bloom admitted paying Stein and the others more than $2 million in money and gifts in return for them using their official positions to award contracts to Bloom and his companies. Bloom, Stein, and the others also facilitated numerous wire transfers of money that were the proceeds of the fraudulently awarded bids and at least $2 million in stolen money from the CPA, in order to conceal the source and origin of the funds. Bloom, a U.S. citizen, is a construction contractor, who had been living in Romania before his arrest on 17 December 2005. His Romanian partners have denied all knowledge of his Iraq activities.
>
> A summary of the Bloom/Stein conspiracy was published by the Special Inspector General for Iraq Reconstruction as an appendix to [h]is October 30, 2006 Quarterly Report to the United States Congress. The conspiracy is estimated to have defrauded the Coalition Provisional Authority of more than $8.6 million.
>
> On February 16, 2007, Bloom was sentenced to 46 months in jail with probation following his sentence as part of a deal for cooperating with the investigation.[1]

I spoke with CPT Cooper following his redeployment and demobilization. I was curious to learn what had become of the soldier he sent back to the U.S. for psychological evaluation, treatment, and discharge from the Army. The soldier had not actually been a member of the Iowa National Guard. He was a soldier from another state's national guard. He had been transferred into CPT Cooper's company at the mobilization station. When the soldier arrived at Ft. Riley, Kansas, for psychological evaluation and out-processing, his paperwork did not accompany him. The story he gave to the cadre at the mobilization station is that he had been returned to CONUS (the continental United States) in order that he might transfer from the National Guard to the active component and serve in the regular Army. When CPT Cooper and his battalion returned to the mobilization station, they were not in time to intervene and prevent this action. The soldier had been transferred to an active duty unit in the Army.

Surviving war is not simply a matter of physical safety. Many soldiers are killed psychologically or spiritually. The mission of chaplains in the U.S. Army is to see that no one is killed because he or she loses his or her moral bearing. Staying alive ethically and morally is not a matter of luck or chance, as is returning home physically unharmed. MG Laich's three "tests" of ethical correctness truly are a helpful starting point in moral self-examination. Would I take this action if my wife and children were watching me? Would I be comfortable reading a factual account of what I had done on the front page of the *Boston Globe*? Would I be secure in knowing that the person who witnessed what I had done is my worst enemy?

War is an incredibly fantastic experience if one lives through it. I wonder, however, if any of us actually live through it. I wonder if one doesn't die a little when a friend is blown up in a car bomb. I wonder if one doesn't die a little when an innocent fellow in the wrong place, at the wrong time, and going in the wrong direction is shot and killed. I wonder if one doesn't die a little when one loses his or her moral bearing. I wonder if one doesn't die a little when a sick soldier cuts off the head and paws of a child's pet. I wonder if one doesn't die a little when a mother is sitting on her front steps weeping and asking why U.S. soldiers hate pets.

Chapter 18

Chaplain (Colonel) Ken Sampson

U.S. Army

If I were to ask what type of soldiers you imagine are promoted in the U.S. Army as chaplains, how would you respond? Would you say that they are the hard-charging, fire-breathing, snake-eating type? That's the answer I would probably have given as a brand-new first lieutenant when I attended my chaplain basic course in 1982. Actually, the Army does admire those traits in its chaplains at certain times. However, if one would like to have a long and distinguished career in today's Army, a different set of characteristics will be required. Chaplains who "charge in where angels fear to tread" don't last very long in the Army. When I look at the Chaplain Corps today, I see that the chaplains who have been promoted to senior positions have a different set of traits.

The person who epitomizes for me what the Chaplain Corps is looking for in its senior officers is CH (COL) Ken Sampson. Ken and I were classmates together in our basic course at Ft. Monmouth, New Jersey. Following our basic course, Ken entered active duty while I joined the Army Reserve. Nevertheless, our paths crossed many times over the course of our careers. The first impression one gets from looking at Ken is that he is a "tall drink of water." He stands head and shoulders above everyone around him. His stature makes him appear dominating, but that belies his personality. He is lanky and moves with a slow, steady gait. He possesses the warm and friendly countenance of a teddy bear. I have actually never seen him without a smile. There is also an air about Ken that elicits trust. The most accurate way to describe Ken Sampson is to say that he has a Jimmy Stewart–like quality about him.

While today's Chaplain Corps desires officers who are circumspect, today's Army desires soldiers who don't make mistakes. Today's Army wants soldiers who don't embarrass themselves, the Army, or the United States, soldiers who are as quick thinking as they are quick on the trigger. It rewards those who are considerate in their deliberations and careful in their actions and doesn't have room for those who make mistakes or public blunders. I am generalizing, of course, and there are always exceptions to the rule, but today's general officers are the ones who are promoted to positions of greater and greater responsibility by being tactically proficient and politically correct.

✠

Today's Army operates under what might best be described as a zero-defect mentality. The United States no longer just goes to war with personnel and equipment. Today's Army goes to war with embedded reporters. The modern battlefield has become a reality show that is broadcast live. Every action by every combatant is scrutinized and replayed in slow motion. The actions of commanders at every echelon are broadcast on the news with "film at eleven." Every minor miscue is portrayed as a major catastrophe.

Senior leaders in the Army know that their military careers can be over in the blink of an eye if "Private Snuffy" does the wrong thing.

To counteract the potential for soldiers to err in judgment or action, senior commanders publish more and more guidance for their troops. The zero-defect mentality pervades today's Army as commanders attempt to mitigate everything that might possibly go wrong and, therefore, put an abrupt end to their careers. Perhaps the following illustration will highlight what I mean.

The U.S. Army is guided by ARs (Army Regulations). AR 670-1 is entitled the "Wear and Appearance of Army Uniforms and Insignia." AR 670-1 is 362 pages in length and tells one everything that one needs to know about the proper wear of the uniform. Well, it tells one almost everything that one needs to know about the wear and appearance of the uniform. During my mobilization and deployment to Kuwait in 2006–2007, CFLCC (Combined Forces Land Component Command) found it necessary to publish an eighteen-page addendum to AR 670-1. You have got to be kidding me! Many senior leaders find it necessary to regulate every moment of their troops' lives from the moment they wake up in the morning until they fall asleep at night. Oh, they also tell them when and where they can sleep as well.

Unfortunately, it is just not possible to soldier-proof the army. Soldiers keep inventing new ways to "make the evening news." One erstwhile soldier decided that it would be a good idea to bring a hand grenade home with him from his tour in Iraq. He actually made it as far as customs at Ali Al Salem Airbase in Kuwait. He had wrapped the grenade in a sock and placed it inside a boot at the bottom of his duffel bag.

All military and civilian personnel returning from deployment must pass through customs prior to departure from theater. A Navy customs team checks and rechecks every item being loaded on planes bound for the United States.

One at a time, every bag, box, suitcase, and carry-on is unpacked in front of an onlooking customs agent. The bags are also scanned to pick up any unauthorized items.

Needless to say, the grenade did not make it onto the plane. One shudders to think what could have happened if this explosive device had detonated in transit! It could very well have brought down the plane, killing all onboard. The ensuing investigation would then bring down everyone in that soldier's chain of command, the commander of the Navy Customs Team, and the senior military leadership in the headquarters that had oversight for Navy Customs. The ripple effect would have been enormous.

The zero-defect mentality in the U.S. Army means that commands and commanders are continually spun up over the most trivial and not-so-trivial actions and events of subordinate units and soldiers.

✠

I was sent to Rosey Rhodes (Roosevelt Rhodes Naval Base, Puerto Rico) for an exercise in 1990. The exercise was a joint training event for the Army, Navy, and Marine Corps. I am not certain if the Air Force and Coast Guard were involved. What I do know is that I arrived on the ground to find chaos. The billeting arrangements for arriving personnel were in disarray. No one knew where he or she was supposed to sleep or eat. Military personnel were headed in a thousand different directions at cross-purposes. And everywhere one looked life was in turmoil.

It was in the midst of this sea of confusion that I spied a lone beacon of calm. It was my friend Ken Sampson. I hadn't seen him in the couple of years since we had attended the Chaplain Advanced Course together. All around him on a sun-drenched field soldiers from a dozen units were in a quandary trying to figure out what they were supposed to be doing. Ken, on the other hand, was taking this opportunity to quiet himself, and he appeared genuinely amused at what was transpiring all around him. It was an incredible portrait of calm under fire. I walked over to Ken and was greeted by his friendly smile and tranquil demeanor. After only a few moments in his presence, I was relieved of my anxiety and agitation.

✠

Over the past twenty or so years, I have discovered my rule of life. My rule of life is not something that I have imposed upon myself from without but something I have discerned lying within me. What I have discovered about myself is that when I am living my rule of life I am in harmony with myself, others, and God.

My rule of life consists of five points. The first is that it is more important to be loving than it is to be right. The second point is that what other people say and do is a statement about them; how I respond is only and always a statement about me. The third is that a static cannot create a dynamic—or, as a seminary professor of mine used to say, "A man has to stand in one place with his mouth open for a long time before a roast duck will fly into it." The fifth is that I am no longer willing to cooperate with those who seek to diminish me or another.

It is the fourth point of my rule of life that I believe has been most helpful in my development as a chaplain in the U.S. Army: I desired to be a nonanxious presence in the world. While everything around me is in confusion and chaos, I can best serve my commander by continuing to be a voice of reason and calm in the midst of upheaval. I have learned that the people with whom I have served are not edified or empowered when I become all spun up along with them.

My CG (commanding general) in Kuwait requested that I begin each day with him and his primary staff at 0730 hours by providing a thought for the day. I based each week's daily thoughts on a theme. The Desert Fathers (early Christian monks living in the desert) was a theme that I believed apropos for those of us spending a year in the desert of Kuwait.

Allow me to digress for a moment regarding the desert of Kuwait. Do you know that there is a port in Kuwait that only imports one item? Can you imagine what that item might be? It's sand! The sand in Kuwait is not of high enough quality to be used in building. All the sand in Kuwait that is used in construction must be imported. You've gotta love the irony of importing sand into the desert!

Anyway, the Desert Fathers were known for their insight and wisdom. My favorite thought for the day during my week on the Desert Fathers is from Abba Pambo (Father Pambo):

> The Archbishop Theophilus made his way to the cell of Abba Pambo, a man recognized and acclaimed for his humility and wisdom. The brethren who accompanied Theophilus said to Abba Pambo, "Say something to the archbishop, so that he may be edified." Abba Pambo replied: "If he is not edified by my silence, he will not be edified by my speech."[1]

I found it helpful in my duties as the chaplain for the Coalition Provisional Authority not to permit myself to be continually spun up at every crisis that appeared on the horizon. If those around me could not be edified by my silence (i.e., my nonanxious presence), they were certainly not going to be enlightened by anything I might say!

Colonel Dennis Sabal, USMC, served as the chief of staff for the Coalition Provisional Authority. Actually, he was the fourth or fifth chief of staff for the CPA during my tenure in Baghdad. Prior to his appointment as chief of staff, however, he came into my office to discuss this possible appointment. There were two things that were important to him: He wanted me to assist him in discerning if this was the work to which God was calling him. And he wanted me to pray with him as he attempted to understand God's will for his life at that moment.

I have been an ordained minister in the church for thirty-four years. I have served congregations for thirty of those years and have served in the military for twenty-five years. When Dennis Sabal walked into my office and asked me to pray with him, it was the only time in my entire ordained life that anyone has asked me to help discern God's direction with regard to potential employment. It was a most profound moment for me. I am not certain why Dennis asked me to pray with him. Maybe it was because I was the CPA chaplain. Maybe it was because he is a faithful Christian. Or maybe it was because, in the midst of the chaos in Baghdad, Dennis needed to spend time with someone who was a nonanxious presence and could help him hear the voice of God in the din of war.

The Army is not looking for chaplains who are hard-charging, fire-breathing snake eaters. The Army is seeking individuals who are a respite of tranquility in the eye of the storm. Senior chaplains in the Army are those who do not exacerbate an already toxic environment. The Army is looking for the Chaplain Ken Sampsons of the world. When I stop to consider it, I believe that is exactly what the church is looking for in its senior leaders as well.

Ft. Bragg, North Carolina, is home to the Army's 18th Airborne Corps and the 82nd Airborne Division. One of the roads on post has a large billboard that says something to the effect that all soldiers on Ft. Bragg will get a day off when the post goes for a specified number of days without an accident or injury. I don't remember if it is ninety or one hundred and twenty days accident free that entitles everyone to a day off. What I do know is that no one has ever gotten a day off!

I was sent to Baghdad as a representative of the CENTCOM Chaplain. I was to provide him with "situational awareness" on the work of the CPA and the need for religious support. The difficulty was that the religious support section that I headed was never officially assigned or attached to the CPA. This meant that the CPA had no responsibility to support our section's mission. I didn't have authorization for a vehicle or a computer or an office. The CENTCOM Chaplain, on the other hand, didn't believe that he had any responsibility to support our team because we were in Baghdad. It was a catch-22. We were caught between "I-raq and a hard place"! I guess I could have started yelling and screaming as a senior field-grade officer, but that didn't seem appropriate. Baghdad was chaotic enough without having the CPA chaplain go haywire. What I did was to begin by writing a prayer. I wanted to center myself for the mission and not lose track of the big picture in the midst the frustrations of daily life in a combat zone. At first, I wanted to entitle it the CPA prayer, but that suggestion was rejected. Instead, I just wrote it out and posted it in English and Arabic on the doors of the chapel:

> Lord of Heaven and Earth,
>
> Throughout the ages you have sent prophets and messengers to reveal your compassion and love to the world and to set your people free from the bondage that enslaves them. We thank you for those who have shown forth your justice, mercy, and righteousness to the people of Iraq. We thank you that through them we have been set free from ignorance and deprivation.
>
> Gracious God, assist us to be messengers of sound government and democracy in your world. Help us in building up that which is good and tearing down that which is decayed. Allow us to share with our brothers, the Iraqis of this land, the manifold gifts that you have bestowed upon us. And, in your good time grant that every person may be freed from fear and poverty and restored to perfect human dignity.
>
> Allow us, Lord, to work with the honorable people of Iraq to build this country, its history, and its future once again.
>
> This we pray in your most gracious name. Amen.

The prayer I originally wrote was not gender specific and had no reference to "our brothers, the Iraqis of this land." Our translators determined that I needed to make the prayer masculine specific in order to resonate with Iraqi culture. I was also intent on remembering that the prophets were instrumental in revealing God's desire to free God's people from bondage. Ezekiel, Daniel, and 2nd Isaiah had proclaimed the message of God's deliverance in what is now Iraq. It was important for me to acknowledge that our mission of freeing the Iraqi people from bondage was rooted in their forebears and received by us as a gift. We were simply returning the "trust" we had received from them:

> We thank you for those who have shown forth your justice, mercy, and righteousness to the people of Iraq. We thank you that through them we have been set free from ignorance and deprivation.

CH (COL) Ken Sampson served as the Joint Task Force Chaplain in Afghanistan during the time that I was deployed to Iraq. I never got the opportunity to see him during the year I spent in Baghdad. I was fortunate enough to see him during his visit to Kuwait in 2007. He had come to support subordinate unit chaplains and chaplain assistants. He came by my office to bring me greetings. His personality hadn't changed a bit. He was still that tall drink of water with a friendly countenance. I don't believe that I ever took the opportunity to tell him what a great mentor he had been to me throughout my military career.

Chapter 19

Hadeel

Am I a person of courage? This is the great existential question of my life. It is something I've wondered about since I was a youngster.

Maybe the reason this question has confronted me my entire life is because I was such a scaredy-cat as a child. I lived in terror of the creatures that hid under my bed at night after the lights had been turned out. I even had a special way of tucking my sheets in around me to prevent these demons from reaching up from under my bed and grabbing me. On the nights that tucking in the sheets properly didn't work to calm my fears, I would slip out of bed and tiptoe down the hall to my sister's room and climb in bed with her. Meg was two years my younger, but I always felt safe when I was with her. Of course, she didn't like having me disturb her sleep and would always ask, "What are you doing here?" And then, "Go back to your own room!"

I would always respond, "I'm here to protect you."

My fear of the dark ended at the age of eleven. I know this because I joined the Boy Scouts at that age and had to memorize the Scout Law. A scout is trustworthy, loyal, helpful, friendly, courteous, kind, obedient, cheerful, thrifty, brave. . . . A scout is supposed to be brave. It wasn't that I was a Scout and a Scout is brave, therefore, I am brave. It was that I was a Scout and one of the attributes of a Scout is bravery. It was time that I began to act like a Scout. The night that it dawned on me that I was expected to be brave was the night that my fear of the dark evaporated. I pulled the sheets out from around my body in the secret way that kept me safe from the creatures under my bed, rolled over, and went to sleep.

I was never again afraid in my darkened room at night. I never again got up and went into my sister's room to "protect her." When I determined to behave like a brave Boy Scout, I became a brave Boy Scout.

✣

My cousin Bob Warnick served in the 101st Airborne during World War II. He wasn't in Easy Company, like the fellows in the HBO miniseries, but he was part of the "band of brothers" that jumped into Normandy and fought at the Battle of the Bulge. Shortly before I deployed to Bosnia, my cousin Bob and his wife came to visit me. He had come to see me in part because he was concerned for my safety in Bosnia.

I thought to myself, "He's worried about me being deployed to Bosnia on a peacekeeping mission? This guy survived some of the most significant combat engagements of the Second World War! What I'm about to endure is nothing compared to what he lived through in Bastogne." I asked him what it was like fighting against the German army during the Battle of the Bulge.

All he would say is, "None of us thought we would live through it." Now, that's courage! It is one thing to place oneself in harm's way believing that one will live through it. It is quite another thing to place oneself in harm's way believing that there is no way one will survive.

✢

On 18 January 2004 at 0800 hours a huge explosion rocked the palace. I was in the midst of the Episcopal-Lutheran-Anglican service when the explosion occurred. I quickly glanced out at the congregation and noticed people cringing. I then peeked up at the ceiling to make certain that it was not collapsing. Nothing was falling down around me, so I continued the prayer uninterrupted.

The explosion that had shaken the palace felt like a bomb must have been just outside building or somewhere behind us inside the palace. In reality, the explosion had been a car bomb just outside the Green Zone near the Assassin's Gate checkpoint. It was a mile from the palace. I could hardly believe that the explosion was that far away. It must have been a tremendous blast.

In my daily journal for that day, I wrote the following:

> It was a tragic day at the CPA today. At 0800 [hours] there was an incredible explosion at the Assassin's Gate. The body count may not be complete, but the number [reported] on TV ranged between 18 and 23. I was in the midst of the prayer of consecration when the blast shook the north end of the palace. The palace is a mile from the explosion.
>
> Andrew White was here this morning. He had passed through the Assassin's Gate 45 minutes before the car bomb was detonated. I am afraid that we will have another memorial service soon. I can't imagine that we didn't lose someone today, either an Iraqi or an American working for the CPA.

✢

Iraqis who worked for the Coalition Provisional Authority placed themselves in danger continually. Some were stalked. Some were threatened. Others were beaten. And still others were shot and killed. There were Iraqis who worked for the CPA who had to keep that information secret even from their own families because family members despised American soldiers and our presence in Iraq.

One Iraqi woman was killed by an IED (improvised explosive device) while traveling in a car with a team of people from one of the CPA ministries. The Iraqis who worked for the CPA did so through an Iraqi contractor. The contractor served as a personnel manager, hiring and firing the Iraqis employed at the palace. The contractor was responsible for hiring individuals who met the qualifications established by the CPA, but the CPA left the management of those hired to the contractor.

The Iraqi contractor did not provide benefits to his employees like health care or life insurance. If an Iraqi was injured or killed in the performance of his or her duties, there was no safety net for income replacement. The contractor was not responsible to assist the family in the event that an employee was killed. Since the CPA had made the contractor responsible for its employees, the CPA itself did not have any fiduciary responsibility to Iraqis working at the palace.

It was customary for individuals from the CPA to contribute money, which was given to the families of Iraqis killed while working for the Coalition Provisional Authority. I remember a number of occasions on which more than two hundred dollars was collected for the families of deceased Iraqi CPA employees. That may not seem like very much money to Americans, but since one U.S. dollars was the equivalent of 14,000 Iraqi dinars, it was not an insignificant amount to present to the family.

A young woman had died, and the members of the ministry in which she worked collected money for her family. They drove into Baghdad, found the family home, and proceeded to give the money to the family. When the mother of the young woman came to the door, she spit on the Americans, took the money, and threw it back in their faces. Not only had the young Iraqi woman placed herself in danger by coming to work at the palace, but she was scorned by her family. Now that took courage!

✝

My mother and sister visited my cousin Bob and his wife between the end of my tour in Iraq and the beginning of my tour in Kuwait. They were coming to New England because the Warnicks live in New Hampshire. My mother and sister would be visiting for a few days, so I invited them to come to the headquarters of the 94th Regional Readiness Command at Ft. Devens, Massachusetts. I had also learned that the CG (Commanding General) would be in the building the day they visited, and I got us on his calendar so that cousin Bob could have some face time with him.

We had a lovely visit with MG Laich, and he was most gracious, especially to my cousin Bob. The CG was spellbound listening to him talk about his years as a soldier. Before we left his office, the CG handed Bob one of his command coins. My mother, sister, Bob, and his wife were about to leave the building when Bob said, "I'll have to put this [the coin] with my other Army awards."

To that I responded in jest, "You mean your three attaboys and a well done?" His wife Marianne turned and said pointedly, "No he means his two Bronze Stars and his Silver Star!" My cousin Bob wasn't just a combat veteran of Normandy and the Battle of the Bulge, he had been awarded medals for valor in combat operations.

✠

Hadeel was an Iraqi who worked for the CPA in one of the ministries. She was twenty-five years of age and engaged to be married. She was petite and had an infectious smile. She was one of the Iraqi Christians who attended Sunday services in the palace and participated in the services by reading the lessons appointed for the day. She read these in Arabic. One of the things that never dawned upon me until I was deployed to Iraq was that the name Allah is not the Muslim word for God. It is the Arabic word for God. Whether one is a Muslim, a Christian, or perhaps even an Arab Jew, God is Allah.

The day before the huge explosion outside the Assassin's Gate I saw Hadeel at a memorial service we were having in the palace for her friend, Nahla Waheed. Nahla had been killed by an IED (improvised explosive device). She had been sitting in the back of a CPA vehicle in between two men returning from one of the Iraqi government buildings when the IED detonated. No one else in the vehicle was injured, but a piece of shrapnel struck her in the back of her head just below her Kevlar helmet. Ambassador Bremer and a member of Nahla's family had participated in the service, and the entire ceremony was quite moving. Nahla was a Muslim, but the memorial services we conducted at the palace tended to be ecumenical in nature. We always managed to integrate readings from the Bible and the Qur'an into the services, and we always began them in the same way, with the first six lines from the Qur'an: "In the name of Allah, Most Gracious, Most Merciful. Praise be to Allah, the Cherisher and Sustainer of the worlds; Most Gracious, Most Merciful; Master of the Day of Judgment. Thee do we worship, and Thine aid we seek. Show us the straight way, the way of those on whom Thou has bestowed Thy Grace, those whose [portion] is not wrath, and who go not astray." It was explained to me by one of the Muslims who helped me conduct memorial services by chanting portions of the Qur'an that these verses (*sura*) were recited for those who had been martyred in the name of Allah. The Iraqis are convinced that anyone killed by terrorists while they are engaged in the effort to rebuild their country is a martyr. Nahla's memorial service began with the first six lines from the Qur'an because she was considered a martyr.

At 0800 hours on 18 January 2004, Hadeel was killed by the suicide bomber at the Assassin's Gate. She was in the rear of a vehicle waiting in line at a checkpoint established to enter the Green Zone. The car in which she was a passenger was only two cars ahead of the suicide bomber's car. The blast from the explosion created so much heat that all the cars around it ignited instantly. The doors on the car in which Hadeel was a passenger welded shut. She never had a chance to escape that blazing inferno and was burned to death.

Democracy in Iraq is being bought for a price. That price is not only being paid with the lives of coalition military personnel. It is being paid with the lives of people like Nahla and Hadeel . . . thousands of Nahlas and Hadeels. Now that's courage!

Winning the major combat operations in Iraq was made possible because of the valor of America's and our coalition partners' young men and women. Winning the peace in Iraq will only be made possible because of the valor of Iraq's young men and women.

I am not certain that I will ever answer the great existential question of my life. I do not really know if I am a person of courage or not. I do know that it is not a question that another can answer for me.

There is one other thing I know. The Army expects all its soldiers to have courage. I know this because the Army has what it terms Army Values. Seven values sum up the attributes of a soldier. They are loyalty, duty, respect, selfless service, honor, integrity, and personal courage. Perhaps I merely need to take a page from the book of my childhood. Perhaps courage is a decision to be made, not a feeling to be achieved. Perhaps I only need to act with the personal courage of a soldier to become a soldier with courage.

Chapter 20

Sheikh Fuad Rashid

The most impressive thing to me about Arab Muslim men, as a chaplain and person of faith, is that they are always praying. I am not referring to the prayers that they pray five times a day as one of the pillars of the Muslim religion. I am referring to the set of prayer beads that Muslim men carry with them and finger while walking or waiting in line or standing on a street corner. In the Arab world, Muslim men pray continually.

I was introduced to Muslim prayer beads while deployed to Bosnia. Our civil affairs team was conducting training for the Turkish brigade in Zenica. The Turks decided to take us to Travnik. Travnik was the capital of Bosnia during the Ottoman Empire and was home to a sixteenth-century mosque. During our tour of this mosque, I saw a basket with sets of prayer beads. I was curious and inquired about them. I was told that strands of Muslim prayer beads are composed of thirty-three beads. There is one bead for each year in the life of Jesus. I was fascinated by the prayer beads and decided to make them part of my religious life. The *mufti* (somewhat akin to a Christian bishop) in Tuzla was kind enough to write out the prayer to be said when using the beads. "God is Great, God is One, Praise be to God, the Master of the Universe."

I discovered during my tour in Iraq that there is more than one type of Muslim prayer beads. Besides the strand with thirty-three beads, there are strands with ninety-nine beads. These prayer beads contain a bead for each of the ninety-nine names of Allah. I was given a strand of the ninety-nine beads by one of the Iraqi Americans working for the Coalition Provisional Authority. He had purchased them on *hajj*. It was humbling for me to be the recipient of such a gift. Muslims prayer beads are made from wood, stone, camel bone, and plastic. They come in all colors and sizes. Some are made from precious stones, and some have inlay. There is one particular kind that is produced from a fragrant rock. One can rub the beads in one's hands and then smell the aroma that is given off. The cords that are used to string the beads together also come in various colors. Some have gold thread intertwined with the string. Vendors can be found in most cities, towns, and villages selling strands of prayer beads. During my year in Iraq, I learned how to "pray the beads" in Arabic.

✣

The Green Zone (now called the International Zone) was the home to not only the Coalition Provisional Authority but quite a few U.S. Army units. The 1st AD (Armor Division) had units stationed within it. U.S. contractors had offices and housing compounds there. There was even a compound for what we referred to as "that three-letter agency" (i.e., the CIA).

The Green Zone was also home to thousands of Iraqis. During the reign of Saddam Hussein, Baathist Party officials lived in and around the Green Zone. One of the areas north of the palace must have been very lovely. Homes were built on a canal that wound its way through the area in a somewhat similar fashion to the River Walk in San Antonio, Texas. The homes had all been abandoned, however. The bombing of the Green Zone prior to the invasion, coupled with the fact that it was the residence of Baathist Party leaders, compelled the residents to flee.

The people living in the Green Zone were probably all squatters who grabbed the opportunity to get ahead in life when the homes there were abandoned. There was no way, however, to prove ownership of the properties, and those Iraqis who were living in the Green Zone when U.S. forces arrived were permitted to stay. Perhaps the Coalition should have forced all Iraqis living within the Green Zone to leave for security purposes. I do believe that those Iraqis who could prove ownership of property were permitted to regain it or they were compensated for it, but my recollection is a bit vague on this point.

✣

The remarkable thing about a democracy is that citizens have the right—no, the duty—to question the actions of their government and its elected officials. We question not only the actions of our government but the motivations of our elected officials that lie behind those actions. American citizens began to raise important questions regarding the hesitation of our longtime allies to support the United States in taking action against Saddam Hussein. Why didn't Germany and France support us? What were we doing wrong?

One of the jokes among military personnel in Iraq is that the U.S. was originally going to call the invasion of Iraq "Operation Iraqi Liberation"—oops, OIL! We can't do that. So we named it Operation Iraqi Freedom.

Citizens in a democracy question the actions of their government. Even military personnel in democratic countries question their governments. What we don't always do in the United States is to question the motivation and actions of our sister states. Perhaps we see it as our responsibility to ask tough questions of our leaders and allow citizens of other democracies to question their own governments. Whatever the case, I sometimes get the impression that U.S. citizens believe that our country's leadership is motivated by less-than-honorable intentions while other nations' leaders are motivated by idealism.

✢

Sheikh (Imam) Fuad Rashid (possible variant spelling—Fouad Rasheed) lived in the Green Zone and was the spiritual leader of a mosque situated there. CH (CPT) Horton introduced me to Sheikh Fuad, whom he had gotten to know when his battalion assumed oversight in area of the Green Zone where the mosque was located and the sheikh lived. Once the U.S. military takes control of an area, the military commander is legally responsible for the well-being of all the people within that area. CH Horton had established contact with Sheikh Fuad on behalf of his commander to ask him to assist in the establishment of security and care for the Iraqis living in that area. CH Horton was anxious for me to meet Sheikh Fuad and escorted me to his home not far from the palace.

I took an immediate liking to Sheikh Fuad. If I were to describe him in two words, they would be *flamboyant* and *outspoken*. I judged him to be about forty years old. He was married to a woman who appeared to be nineteen or twenty. He was fluent in English and a most welcoming host. Sheikh Fuad invited CH Horton and me into his office to talk. The first thing I noticed was a rectangular prayer mat with some sort of contraption at one end. The contraption was a stand about two feet high. Around the stand was a large strand of beads about the size of tangerines. It reminded me of children's pop beads. All of these beads were white, however. The beads hung down both sides of the stand, and a notch at the top of the stand separated the beads on one side from the beads on the other. I asked Sheikh Fuad what this was. He told me that it was a large set of Muslim prayer beads, one thousand in all. Sheikh Fuad used these beads during his daily prayers.

Sheikh Fuad was a Sunni cleric. The mosque in which he served had been a favorite of the Baathist leadership living in the area. Saddam Hussein had prayed there, and Sheikh Fuad knew him personally. Following our conversation, Sheikh Fuad's wife brought us food and something to drink. I had just finished eating lunch and was stuffed, but I didn't want to insult Sheikh Fuad and his wife by not eating. I did manage to eat a little bit, but I could tell that it wasn't enough. Sheikh Fuad keep asking me if I liked what his wife had prepared.

✢

The Believers' Palace was just across the street from Saddam's former presidential palace in Baghdad. It must have been a grand structure at one time, but it had been pretty well demolished in the air attack that proceeded the ground invasion. The Believers' Palace was nothing more than an elaborate hoax. The palace was built to disguise a three-story air-raid shelter located beneath it. In between the palace and the air-raid shelter, piles of rubble and earth had been placed to prevent bombs from penetrating into the shelter. The engineering had worked. Seven two thousand–pound bombs had hit the Believers' Palace, but the air-raid shelter was undamaged. I am certain that the name Believers' Palace and lovely edifice were designed to hide the true intention of the structure.

I was permitted to tour the ruins of the Believers' Palace and the air-raid shelter beneath it. The upper levels of the structure had been destroyed, with gaping holes in the dome. It was possible to imagine, nonetheless, what it must have looked like before it was destroyed. It must have been awe inspiring. One feature of the Believers' Palace was that there were elevator doors like the kind one might find in the lobby of a posh hotel, but they didn't open. It wasn't because the bombing had destroyed them. The elevator doors were part of the building's disguise. There were literally floors and floors of rubble and earth above the air-raid shelter. The Believers' Palace sat a number of stories high on top of the debris used as filler. The elevator doors were constructed to give the impression that one could stop on the floors below.

Under the debris and rubble was the three-story air-raid shelter. It was not possible to tour the entire shelter because electricity to the Believers' Palace had been knocked out during the bombing, and the two lower floors had flooded because the sump pumps weren't working. Nevertheless, the tour was most impressive. The air-raid shelter had dozens of bedrooms with wood-paneled walls. There were kitchens and bathrooms. There was a dispensary and meeting rooms. There was also a large conference room that looked familiar to me. I was certain that Saddam and his cabinet had been seated around the table there during one of the Iraqi television broadcasts prior to the war. I turned out to be correct. It was the place where the cabinet had gathered for safety and security.

There was one other item of note in the air-raid shelter. All of the mechanical devices necessary to make the bunker inhabitable were manufactured in France, Germany, and Russia. The Believers' Palace had been constructed in the midst of the U.N. embargo on Iraq. The materials used to construct the bunker had been smuggled into Iraq in violation of the embargo. Maybe the motivations of some of our sister nations in opposing the invasion of Iraq were not quite as idealistic as we might want to believe. Perhaps it might behoove us to consider the motives of our "friends and allies" before assuming that they acted with right intention while we did not.

I am convinced—no, certain—that if we followed the money, it would be an eye-opening exercise. What did the countries that opposed United Nations intervention in Iraq have to gain? What did European leaders or their family members have to gain personally by resisting intervention in Iraq? Follow the money! Of course, it has also become evident from more recent events in Europe that intervention in Iraq could have created significant internal strife for some countries. I'd follow the money, however.

One of my hopes was that Sheikh Fuad Rashid would work with the CMATT (Coalition Military Assistance Training Team) in providing religious support at Kirkush Military Training Base for soldiers in the new Iraqi army. To that end, I invited Sheikh Fuad to a meeting in my office with other sheikhs to discuss such a plan.

It turned out to be a disaster. A discussion (debate) began between the sheikhs. Sheikh Fuad insisted that "not all Baathists were bad." He claimed that good and evil could be found in all individuals and that it is a mistake to judge everyone based upon whether or not that person was a Baathist. He was correct of course, but he didn't understand the political landscape. The Coalition was not about to send a sheikh to the new Iraqi army training base to inform recruits that the Baathists weren't all that terrible! Sheikh Fuad was shooting himself in the foot, and he couldn't stop himself from talking. I tried to mitigate the damage with a few comments in response to Sheikh Fuad, but it was too late: the damage had already been done. Sheikh Fuad was not selected to assist CMATT.

I was to learn, however, that Sheikh Fuad was just as vocal in his support of the United States. Since he was a Sunni cleric, this was extraordinary. The following is taken from an article about him that was published shortly after I returned to the United States:

> Rashid is imam of the al-Qadisiya Mosque, the sole Muslim house of worship in the Green Zone, the 3-square-mile area in the heart of Baghdad that effectively remains under U.S. control. And despite the criticisms he had just leveled, he proudly calls himself the "only imam in Iraq who speaks in favor of the Americans."
>
> "I love America," Rashid said, with passion. "Americans are so beautiful."
>
> Resplendent in a cream-colored gown and a white gauze turban around his boyish face, the 40-year-old Rashid looks more like a Catholic nun than a Muslim cleric. The similarity is deliberate—he readily admits that he models himself after Mary, the mother of Jesus.

> Although Islamic doctrine considers Mary the virgin mother of a prophet—a status almost as revered in Islam as it is in Christianity—it is unheard of for a Muslim cleric to adopt Christian-style garb, much less a woman's.
>
> Rashid says Mary appeared to him in three visions telling him to follow her. He adopted the style when he was a seminary student in Baghdad in the early 1990s, but it has become more pronounced since his mosque came under U.S. protection after the April 2003 fall of Saddam Hussein's regime.
>
> Rashid's close-cropped beard is dyed blond, in keeping with his all-white image—a sign of purity, he says—and he wears patterned contact lenses.[1]

As I stated earlier, if I were to use two words to describe Sheikh Fuad Rashid they would be *flamboyant* and *outspoken.*

I enjoyed Sheikh Fuad, and I appreciated his openness. He looked forward to the day when all people would be able to come to his mosque and pray. He envisioned Sunni and Shia, Christians, and Jews all gathered together for prayer and worship. His idealism was offset a bit by his comments regarding the Shia, whom he found to be ignorant and filthy liars. It was also tempered by the fact that when he spoke of Jews, he wasn't referring to Zionist Jews (i.e., those desiring a homeland in "Palestine")! Many (perhaps most) Jews would contend that Judaism and Zionism are inseparable and that Sheikh Rashid "just doesn't get it." I grant that Sheikh Fuad was not as enlightened as one might desire, but he was at least intellectually open to a new relationship among Muslims, Jews, and Christians. More importantly, he was willing to put his life on the line by expressing his openness:

> "If he were anywhere else in Iraq, he would be killed," said one Iraqi man who visited the mosque recently and asked to remain anonymous. "And I would do it myself," he added, saying Rashid "gives a bad example."[2]

I really liked Sheikh Fuad Rashid. I liked his flamboyance and political outspokenness. I also liked the fact that he had taught himself English by watching Hollywood movies. On the other hand, I appreciated the fact that he lived humbly and simply. When I was home for my R&R, I decided that I would purchase a DVD player and some movies for Sheikh Fuad and his wife. I found a couple of Pink Panther movies that I thought he'd enjoy. Upon my return to Iraq, I asked CH Horton to accompany me to Sheikh Fuad's home. One afternoon we visited the house, set up the DVD player in the living room, and connected it to the television. Now that I think about it, however, I hope that Sheikh Fuad isn't increasing his English vocabulary by listening to Peter Sellers as Inspector Clouseau!

Chapter 21

Cornelius

Saddam's former presidential palace is situated on a bend in the Tigris River across from the compound in which the Ishtar Sheraton Baghdad and Palestine International hotels are located. Actually, the Sheraton is not owned and operated by the Sheraton Hotels chain but may have been at some point in the past. One may find an apt description of the hotels on the Internet at Yahoo:

> Palestine & Sheraton located across the road from each other in a safe and protected zone. You can only walk between the hotels but do you really need to go out? The standard of the Palestine is YMCA. Basic room with bathroom/shower. Breakfast cereal and eggs and not much else throughout the day. Walk across to the Sheraton for nicer selection. Most of the hotel used by commercial, media and private security organizations so don't be alarmed if you see guns being carried throughout the hotel and lifts. It does get the occasional rocket launched into the side of the hotel but not often enough to worry about. Pretty common for Baghdad. Staff friendly and they have a small shop at reception. These two hotels have been made famous because they serve as the home for the international press corps that live and report from balconies overlooking the city. Adjacent to these hotels is the blue domed mosque that is regularly viewed as the backdrop for live news broadcasts from the city.[1]

One of the criticisms leveled at the international press corps by members of the CPIC (Coalition Press Information Center) (pronounced *cee-pic*) during my time in Baghdad was that many of the reporters never left the safe haven of the hotel. They preferred to convey secondhand information as if they had received it as a firsthand witness. My friends at the CPIC doubted the veracity of much of what was reported by the press as fact. This was true of both the international and domestic news media.

✠

The Blackwater Company provides security for individuals who work and travel in Iraq. They are a sort of mercenary-for-hire organization composed of highly trained and skilled fighters. I doubt that Blackwater executives would describe their company's service as mercenaries-for-hire, but that is the function their company provides. In point of fact, Blackwater is just one of any number of private security firms that provide safety and security services for VIPs working in Iraq. Iraqi government officials generally have security teams composed of individuals from their own tribes and family. International government officials had PSDs (personal security detachments) provided by their own nation's military or international soldiers of fortune working for private security firms. Ambassador Bremer's PSD was composed of former U.S. military personnel and retired law enforcement officers working for Blackwater.

The logistical complications encountered when coordinating meetings of high-level government and nongovernmental officials was always increased because of the PSDs. For example, a meeting of ten VIPs required a venue that could accommodate up to one hundred and twenty people. Event planners needed to take into consideration the additional ten to twelve armed individuals who would accompany each VIP. Unknown armed individuals accompanying VIPs and entering secure buildings posed another set of challenges with regard to event planning.

Prior to my mobilization and deployment to Iraq, I spent the three summers with teams of visitors from the congregation I served. We visited all the homes in our zip code door to door. We actually visited many homes outside our zip code as well. In order to accomplish the neighborhood visitation, we had groups of people go out in small teams. Each of these four teams had a team leader. Two of our teams were led by seminary students whom we hired to work with us during the summer. In the course of three summers, we visited more than thirteen thousand residences. One of the seminary students whom we employed was Mpho (pronounced *umm-paw*) Tutu. Mpho is the daughter of the Nobel Peace Prize Laureate Archbishop Desmond Tutu. One of the wonderful things about Mpho is that she does not get lost in the shadow of her father. She is a very intelligent, insightful, and personable individual who is extremely talented.

Following the first week of our door-to-door visitation, Mpho announced to us all that "daddy" was visiting and then inquired if we could see fit to come to her home one morning instead of going out visiting to share Holy Communion with Desmond. Believe me, it was not a difficult decision to make. Let's see, we could spend three hours knocking on doors in the neighborhood, or we could spend the morning with a Nobel Peace Prize laureate who had helped put an end to apartheid in South Africa. It was a glorious morning at Mpho's home with her father and mother and half a dozen members of our congregation.

Two years later, Mpho came back to work for the congregation as our seminarian associate. I put her to work assisting with the Sunday morning worship and preaching from time to time. The first Sunday Mpho joined us, I asked her to prepare the sermon and lead a portion of the service. We entered the church for her first service and there sat "daddy" in one of the front pews of the church. He had come to support his daughter on her first Sunday as our associate.

✠

The early months in Iraq were relatively peaceful. The population was happy to be rid of Saddam, and there was a great sense of anticipation among the Iraqi people about their future. There was, of course, sporadic violence, and security was always a significant concern. Nevertheless, I was given permission to organize and coordinate weekly trips to the ruins at ancient Babylon. These excursions were conducted on Fridays because it is the Muslim holy day and business was not conducted with Iraqis on that day. Coalition Provisional Authority personnel were given free time on Fridays. A jaunt to Babylon, therefore, fit easily into the weekly routine. The ancient city of Babylon is situated about eighty kilometers south and slightly west of Baghdad on the Euphrates River near the modern city of al-Hillah. A day trip was perfect for traveling to Babylon, taking the tour of the ruins, eating lunch, and returning.

The 1st Marine Expeditionary Force (1-MEF) had established their base of operations at Babylon. This not only afforded security for the archeological site but made it safe for individuals touring the ruins. Chaplain (CDR) Felix Marrerro, 1-MEF command chaplain, had organized tours of the ruins by enlisting the aid of the archeologists who had excavated the site. They had worked for years under the direction of Saddam and were extremely knowledgeable. More importantly, they all had a good command of the English language.

✠

Ambassador Bremer traveled to the United States frequently for meetings with President George Bush, Secretary of Defense Donald Rumsfeld, and other high ranking U.S. officials. Because of this fact, his Blackwater PSD was relatively free for other activities when he was away. One of their personnel approached me and inquired if I would be willing to organized a special trip to the ruins at Babylon for the members of Bremer's PSD. I agreed, and we established 23 October as the date for our excursion because the Ambassador would be out of the country. It was explained to me that we would be traveling in the Ambassador's "hard cars" and that about a dozen people would be going on the tour.

I had never heard of a hard car before being deployed to Iraq. However, in Baghdad we spent a good deal of time at staff meetings discussing hard cars in anticipation of the arrival of Ambassador Bremer and his team from the State Department. Basically a hard car is a vehicle that has been specially outfitted with armor, bulletproof glass, and other features in order to withstand small arms and rifle fire. The Coalition Provisional Authority had ordered eleven such cars for Ambassador Bremer's team. Each hard car cost approximately $250,000.

✠

Besides the International Press Corps that resided at the Palestine and Sheraton hotels across the Tigris River from the presidential palace, there were numerous contractors billeted in support of the U.S. military. Some, I believe, worked for AAFES (Army/Air Force Exchange Service). Among them were a dozen or more individuals who were intent on receiving religious support from us in terms of weekly worship services. Since it was too dangerous and logistically difficult to transport these folks to the presidential palace each Sunday for services, I agreed to conduct a weekly service at the Sheraton Hotel. We would gather on the fifteenth floor of the hotel. The space had once been a grand dining room with floor-to-ceiling plate glass windows so guests could look out over Baghdad. The hotel had, however, become a target for rocket attacks, and the day prior to one of my visits a rocket had crashed into the fifteenth floor, destroying an elevator adjacent to the dining room. We now had to walk up the fifteen flights for worship services.

An IED is an improvised explosive device. IEDs are by far the single most dangerous threat to Coalition military and civilian personnel and are the primary cause of death and injury for U.S. service members. I remember returning to Baghdad from my R&R only to be greeted with a new acronym, VBIED. I knew what an IED was, but what in the world was a VBIED? Did that mean "very bad" IED? It actually refers to a vehicle-borne IED. The rocket that hit the Sheraton Hotel the day prior to my visit had been strapped onto a donkey. I couldn't help but wonder if we'd have a new acronym for that: DBIED! The next day I saw some pictures of the poor terrified beast of burden to which the IED had been attached. His hair was singed and he had a shell-shocked look in his eyes.

The trek across the Tigris was so dangerous that a PSD was assigned to pick me up at the palace and escort me to the compound that contained the Sheraton and Palestine hotels. Two vehicles would come for me along with seven or eight PSD personnel. They would then race through the city and deliver me to the hotel compound. Each time we traveled to or from the hotel, we used a different route as a security precaution. One of the PSD team members was always seated in the third row of the SUV or, as it is known in the military, NTV (nontactical vehicle), to keep an eye out for anyone approaching from the rear with harmful intent. The rest of the team members kept a vigilant 360-degree lookout for anything that appeared suspicious.

Upon our arrival at the compound, the team leader instructed me to remain in the vehicle until the team members had taken up their positions with submachine guns at the ready. Three of the team formed a triangle about twenty feet apart from each other. I was then placed in the middle of this triangle and walked into the hotel. The truth of the matter is that I never felt secure when I traveled with the PSD or was escorted by them into the hotel. I always thought that they drew attention to me and highlighted me as a target. After all, if a terrorist is looking for a target, who is he more apt to target? Will his first inclination be to shoot at a PSD team member or the person they are escorting? I know what I'd do. I'd take out the VIP first.

The day I took Ambassador Bremer's Blackwater PSD to Babylon was an unforgettable experience. I had actually been looking forward to making the trip with a group of former SEALs, Special Forces operatives, and a retired South Carolina state trooper. We would be traveling in hard cars with lots of firepower and highly skilled security personnel who knew exactly how to handle themselves in a firefight. We generally traveled to Babylon in buses with no armor or bulletproof glass. I pitied anyone who might choose to engage this PSD as we traveled to al-Hillah. What I wasn't prepared for was the ride itself. Bremer's PSD drove like maniacs! They swerved in and out of traffic, ignored all traffic lights, and didn't slow down for people walking across the road. By the time we arrived at Babylon, I wanted to get out of the car and kiss the ground. I'd never been so happy to arrive anywhere in my life. Now, if I could only get home in one piece! As far as I was concerned, it was preferable to be rocketed, mortared, IEDed, and shot at by irate Iraqis than to travel in the "safety" of Bremer's PSD.

One of the security detachments that worked at the presidential palace was composed of individuals from South Africa. The Coalition Provisional Authority had a number of ministries that were established to assist in getting the new Iraqi government up and running. There was the Ministry of Interior, the Ministry of Defense, and so on. The South African PSD provided security to the Ministry of Health (MoH) in support of the Provisional Authority. Whenever a ministry VIP traveled in Iraq to meet with an Iraqi counterpart, PSD personnel were present. There were ten or so members of the South African team, and it was evident to me that they had all received military training or had preformed military service in South Africa. The ministry also had a linguist who traveled with the PSD when they escorted someone into the city or surrounding country.

It was a Friday afternoon, and Francois Jacques deBeer, one of the South African PSD team, decided to go into the city to purchase some items for a party that evening. He took the linguist with him to translate. While they were shopping, someone with a pistol approached and shot Francois in the chest four or five times. He died instantly. This was, of course, a shock to the South African PSD team, the members of the Ministry of Health that they supported, and the rest of the Coalition Provisional Authority community. What made the event even more tragic was that Francois, who was in his early forties, had two children, ages seven and nine.

I went to visit the Ministry and the PSD team to see what they would like to do in terms of a memorial service for Francois. They all wanted to have a fitting memorial, and the next day their team leader came to my office to discuss the memorial program. His name was Cornelius, and I observed that he was a very competent leader who cared a great deal for his men. I took an immediately liking to him because of his biblical name. It made sense to me that someone with the name of a Roman centurion should be the head of a PSD. The fact of the matter is that I had memorial services in Baghdad every month on average while I was there. However, the memorial service for this South African PSD member was actually the finest one I conducted. And it wasn't because I did such an outstanding job. It was because Cornelius and the other members of the team helped me to do something appropriate and fitting for their friend and colleague. Because of Cornelius's diligence the memorial service was a suitable tribute.

I always attempt to put people at ease when I meet with them. Cornelius was no exception. I wanted to create a shared bond with him as we worked together to care for those who had been devastated by the death of their team member. So I decided to tell him about my relationship with Mpho Tutu and, therefore, my slight connection to him and the other South African members of his team. I shared with him the occasion when we traveled to Mpho's home and had Holy Communion with Desmond. I told him about Mpho's first service as seminarian associate and Desmond's presence in the congregation. I thought that surely this would help create a good rapport between us. Cornelius listened patiently and attentively. When I was finished, he just sat back in his chair and said matter-of-factly, "Hmm, Desmond Tutu. . . . He was on my hit list, but, of course, that was during apartheid."

I had just met the man whose job it was to assassinate Desmond Tutu if given the order by the South African government. Immediately following my meeting with Cornelius, I sent a note to Mpho informing her that I'd just met the man who was assigned to murder her father when instructed to do so.

Part of the territory that goes along with being a soldier in a combat zone is that one's life is constantly on the line and that death could be just around the next corner. It is for this reason that the U.S. military pays what is called imminent danger pay to anyone serving in harm's way. I expect that in a war I might very well be killed at any time day or night. What I don't often stop to consider is that being an advocate for peace and reconciliation in the world can be just as dangerous a mission as serving in any combat zone.

Chapter 22

Tony Pugliese

Kellogg, Brown, and Root (KBR), a subsidiary of the Halliburton Corporation, was responsible for providing "life support" to U.S. military and civilian personnel in Iraq. KBR built base camps throughout Iraq and then managed the camps they constructed. At Saddam's former presidential palace, KBR provided billeting (housing) and ran the Green Zone shuttle buses and laundry. KBR maintained the palace, provided the food service through a subcontractor, and provided nontactical vehicles (NTVs) for the Coalition Provisional Authority. They ran the fuel point (gas station), the supply store (i.e., computer supplies, fans, mops, etc.), and barber shop. KBR also renovated buildings within the Green Zone that would be required for CPA operations.

The U.S. military has contracted many of the life support functions that used to be provided by the military itself. The military is no longer a self-sufficient organization that can conduct forward-based operations without substantial civilian support. The modern battlefield is a complex interdependency between the U.S. military and corporate America. Convoys that carry troops and supplies throughout the theater of operations are not primarily U.S. assets. Truck and bus drivers from Pakistan, India, and the Philippines are employed to haul personnel and baggage. Former civilian contract employees from Bosnia and Kosovo now work in Iraq, Afghanistan, and Kuwait for the Halliburton Corporation.

Living at the former presidential palace was one continual old home week. Everyday I would bump into someone I knew from a previous deployment. It was not unexpected to bump into friends from the military, but it was a shock to learn that one knew some of the TCNs (third-country nationals) from previous deployments.

✠

KBR established a laundry facility at the palace shortly following our arrival. The laundry operation highlighted for me the unique interaction that exists between the U.S. military, corporate America, and TCNs. Of course, the laundry did have some initial operating challenges. One did not always receive back from the laundry the items that one dropped off a few days earlier. I actually established a "laundry exchange" in the chapel where people could leave things that they'd gotten back in the wash that didn't belong to them and pick up items that looked familiar. I actually went through the year's deployment with someone else's Army T-shirt. I couldn't locate the individual to whom it belonged. Luckily, it was just the right size and the "last four" of the social security number stenciled inside were close to mine!

KBR also began to provide dry-cleaning service. This was particularly important for civilian personnel working at the CPA who had daily interaction with the Iraqi nationals who were helping to build a new government. A friend of mine turned in three new suits at the laundry point but was not informed that the policy had changed and that dry cleaning was no longer provided. His suits were returned washed, dried, and folded! They had also shrunk a bit. Oops! He did file a claim and eventually was reimbursed $1,500.

One of the fellows who worked at the laundry was from Albania. I met him one day while he was tossing bags of clean laundry from the back of a van into the building that served as the laundry point. I engaged him in conversation and asked what he had done in Albania. As it turned out, he was a nationally famous opera singer in his native country. It was more profitable for him, however, to shuttle laundry in Baghdad than it was for him to sing in the Albanian opera. He did end up entertaining some CPA dignitaries on occasion, but his training as an operatic singer was abandoned in favor of this menial chore.

Tony Pugliese was one of the senior managers of KBR at the palace in Baghdad. I met Tony one Sunday morning following our early worship service. During my sermon, I talked about growing up in the Philadelphia area and listening to a rock-and-roll radio station whose call letters were WIBG. I explained in my sermon that the IBG in WIBG stood for "I believe in God."

Tony couldn't wait to talk to me after the service. We had both grown up listening to WIBG and eating Philly cheesesteaks, soft pretzels, and Tastykakes. His favorite Tastykakes were the chocolate ones with the chocolate frosting. I received a Tastykake "care package" from time to time and was always certain to slip into Tony's office when he was out and leave a couple packages of his favorite Tastykakes on his desk. Tony and I were to become good friends during our time in Baghdad. Not only did we share a common heritage, but Tony was also a very dedicated Christian who assisted me during our early morning worship.

I had known KBR as Brown and Root while deployed to Bosnia in 1998–99. Brown and Root coordinated life support services at Eagle Base. They managed the laundry, employed the tradesmen who renovated the base, and hired the linguists who served as our translators. They also ran the DFAC (dining facility).

The DFAC at Eagle Base provided excellent food and was open all day long. If one missed a meal, the sandwich bar was always available. The DFAC also provided special dinners from time to time. The DFAC might have Chinese night or Mexican night. One Thursday afternoon a sign appeared at the entrance to the DFAC that read "Monday will be Native American night." Native American night! What in the world was Native American night? Would we be having corn and buffalo perhaps? Did they intend to serve hamburgers and hot dogs? What in the world would we be having on Monday evening for dinner?

I had completely forgotten about Native American night and wasn't planning on going to dinner that night when I received a knock on my hooch door. It was Dick Buck, our detachment commander. Had we been to the DFAC? We had to get up there right away and experience Native American night. My roommate and I hurried off to the DFAC. We arrived and were greatly surprised. Someone must have explained to the Bosnians running the DFAC that Native Americans are Indians. We found such "Native American" dishes as curried chicken and Bombay rice! The Bosnians working in the DFAC seemed shocked that all of us Americans did not particularly like "Native American" food. Working in a multinational environment can and does create cultural disconnects occasionally.

The first shuttle bus from the Al-Rasheed Hotel to the palace left at 0530 hours daily. I always made certain to take the first shuttle bus for a number of reasons. First, the Al-Rasheed always ran out of hot water. Getting up early assured me hot water (well, most of the time). Second, the little buses that were used for shuttling people back and forth to the palace didn't have air conditioners sufficient to cope with the heat of the Baghdad day. Catching the shuttle bus prior to sunrise ensured a pleasant ride. Finally, the early morning shuttle bus was not particularly crowded. All in all, it was worth the effort of getting up early for the first shuttle bus of the day. I'd generally stand outside the hotel with eight or nine others waiting for the bus to arrive and then sit on it for five or ten minutes before it departed. The bus driver was a British fellow who loved listening to BBC radio. BBC News was always playing throughout the bus as we awaited our departure. Occasionally BBC radio would do an exposé on some bizarre topic as we sat at the bus stop.

Chief Michael Lines of the U.S. Navy served as one of my chaplain assistants (in the Navy they are not chaplain assistants, but RPs) during my tour in Iraq. I actually had four different assistants during my year deployed. There was Master Sergeant Dave Gagnon, who had helped to bring me on active duty. Then there were three Navy chiefs: Chief Dexter Johnson followed Chief Lines. Chief Vincent Sievers arrived shortly before I returned to the U.S.

Chief Lines and I rode the early bus together from the Al-Rasheed to the palace. One morning as we were waiting to depart for the palace the BBC presented a story on yoiking. *Yoiking* is a type of Scandinavian folk music that sounds very much like a cross between hog calling and yodeling. Here I was sitting at a bus stop in Baghdad, Iraq, listening to BBC radio while some Scandinavian folk musician was yoiking! I was a cultural Alice in Wonderland. The early morning "yoik" became a little source of amusement for Chief Lines and me. He had the good fortune to complete his tour prior to Thanksgiving in 2003 and return home. To show him that I had not forgotten him I sent him a yoiking CD at Christmas.

The bus stop outside the Al-Rasheed Hotel didn't last too long. One afternoon a mortar or rocket made a direct hit on it. The gaping hole in the ground and the burning wood of the bench and floorboards of the bus stop convinced me that taking the 0530 hours bus had been an astute decision for this additional reason.

KBR does not hire chaplains to provide religious support to their personnel. Tony Pugliese did, however, contact me on numerous occasions to provide pastoral counseling to individuals working for KBR. People who are away from their families for a year or more do have crises. They experience deaths in their families. They go through divorces. Many KBR employees have taken jobs in combat zones because of financial problems that remain unresolved. While deployed, KRB employees have fellow employees that are killed. They too live in harm's way and must cope with the fears that accompany life in a combat zone.

The IED attack that occurred on our last trip to the ruins at ancient Babylon did not hit our bus. Luckily, it just missed us. It did, however, take the bumper off the KBR vehicle following the bus. The woman driving the vehicle was shaken by the experience. Tony approached me and requested that I spend some time talking to her. Prior to my departure from Baghdad, another KBR senior representative in Iraq approached me. KBR was wanting to know if I'd be interested in remaining in Iraq as a civilian chaplain and working for them.

It had become evident to some of the senior KBR management in Iraq that providing religious support to their personnel was imperative for the accomplishment of their mission. I did speak with a representative, but KBR did not end up hiring a chaplain to provide religious support for their personnel.

Over the past decade or so in the United States, we have been inundated with news stories regarding the abuse of children who work in "sweatshops" producing goods for Americans. The American public has reacted to these revelations with revulsion, and rightly so. There is something else equally shocking, but not quite so evident, that escapes our attention. When we establish sweatshops and employ children to work in them, we alter what another culture deems valuable.

Let me explain it this way. The palace in Baghdad had a barbershop located not far from the south portico. That barbershop employed four or five barbers who probably earned very little an hour. Had their plight been aired on U.S. television, Americans would probably be aghast. How could we in good conscience employ Iraqis to work in the palace and pay them so little? Actually, all haircuts were free at the palace barbershop. What we all did, therefore, was to tip the barbers a dollar each for a haircut. The barbershop was always packed, and the barbers were working nonstop all day long. Let's suppose for a moment that a barber does four haircuts an hour. That individual would then receive over thirty dollars in tips for a day's work. One U.S. dollar is equal to 14,000 Iraqi dinars. A day's work for a barber paid that individual over 420,000 dinars a day. Multiply that amount by five, and one can see that two million dinars a week is not out of reach for a barber.

What do you suppose was the average pension for Iraqis who were doctors and lawyers? The CPA increased their pensions from 24,000 dinars per month under Saddam to 150,000 dinars. Iraqi professionals living on pensions received almost nothing in comparison to barbers working at the CPA. I am fairly certain that Iraqi doctors don't earn nearly as much as the day workers cleaning the palace.

The problem of "sweatshops" is not merely that children are making a pittance for their labor. The problem is that we are contributing to a shift in societal values that makes working in a shoe factory or knitting mill preferable to professions that contribute to the enhancement of civilization. Sweatshops aren't just a problem because they help to create an environment abusive to children; they are a problem because they devalue those things that are required for the advancement of human society. Why should one be a doctor when he or she can earn much more money sitting at a sewing machine?

✝

Another of the corporate compounds within the Green Zone belonged to Bechtel. Bechtel employees had their own containerized living compartments. They had containerized offices, but more importantly Bechtel had their own dining facility with their own contracted kitchen staff. The meals at the DFAC in the palace tended to be frozen foods that were fried. The food at Bechtel was worthy of the finest restaurants in the U.S.

CH Ken Beale from the Air Force joined our ministry team at the palace shortly before my tour ended. Ken was a Roman Catholic priest who discovered that the senior member of Bechtel in Baghdad was a member of his congregation at the palace. We, therefore, got invited to dinner at the Bechtel compound on two separate occasions. On one of the two occasions, the entrees were beef tenderloin and lobster. The desserts were heavenly!

✝

It was a pleasure to work with Tony Pugliese because he had a genuine concern for his subordinates at KBR in Baghdad. It was also a pleasure to work with Tony because of his military background. He understood the military system and was able to integrate his knowledge of the civilian and military sectors into an efficiently run organization. There was one other thing I liked about Tony. He had paid his dues in regard to serving our country. He had spent more than twenty years in the Air Force.

It is widely understood by U.S. military personnel deployed to Iraq today that one can earn far more money working as a contractor than serving in the military. And if one is working for Bechtel, then he or she will also enjoy fine dining. Many of our brightest and best commissioned and noncommissioned officers are choosing to leave the military after their initial term of service is completed and return to theater as civilian contractors. They can earn two or three times their military pay and are also entitled to the tax exemption for serving in a combat zone.

I wonder what the cultural demise is to a society that values "sweatshops" to medicine. I wonder what happens when it is far more advantageous for a population to sew denim jeans for generations of Americans than it is to become part of a rising middle class. I also wonder what happens to a society that places a much higher economic value on contracted services than it does on duty to country.

Chapter 23

Hamid al-Sharifi

I traveled into Kuwait City from Camp Arifjan for a dinner meeting shortly after my arrival at Camp Arifjan. It was my first visit to the city since I'd left in 2004 on my way home from Iraq. I called up to the room of the person with whom I'd be meeting and was standing by the registration when I was approach by an Arab gentleman. He looked at me and asked, "Aren't you Frank Wismer?" I was shocked. How in the world would an Arab in Kuwait City have the faintest idea of who I was?

"Yes," I said and extended my hand to shake his.

Then he asked, "Do you know who I am?"

Isn't it awful when someone knows you and expects that you should know them, but you don't have a clue? I fumbled for a few moments and then had to admit that I did not know his name. He said, "I'm Hamid al-Sharifi. I used to visit your office in the palace in Baghdad with Andrew White and Georges Sada. You let me use your computer."

"Hamid," I said, "this is a wonderful surprise! It's great to see you again. Tell me, what are you doing in Kuwait City?"

Hamid replied, "I am the Iraqi Ambassador to Kuwait. I have a reception to attend this evening here at the hotel."

Military chaplains have two distinct job requirements. They are expected to serve both as pastors and as staff officers. The more senior a chaplain becomes, the more he or she is expected to be a good staff officer. Senior chaplains are expected to conduct strategic planning and assist their commanders in understanding the religious landscape of the area of responsibility (AOR). When I deployed to Iraq, I made up my mind that I would begin my work as a pastoral presence and then branch out into my other areas of responsibility as I became more comfortable with the Coalition Provisional Authority and its structure.

I always wondered, nevertheless, if I had approached my position in the proper manner. Should I have spent less time as a pastor and more time as a staff officer? The answer to my question had just been given. Because I had chosen to be a pastor first and staff officer second, I had developed a number of significant relationships during my year in Iraq.

One notable difference between American and Arab culture is that Arabs spend time developing relationships while Americans are intent on the task at hand. We're all about conducting business. Arabs develop relationships first. It is not uncommon when doing business with an Arab to spend an hour talking about family—always family first—then life in general, and finally the matter at hand. There are occasions when one isn't even certain if any business will get conducted at all. It is almost as if it is an afterthought. Then at the last moment the business to be conducted is mentioned.

✠

The Coalition Provisional Authority hired hundreds of day workers. One group of day workers cleaned the palace and the bathroom units outside. Another group of day workers assembled hooches (living containers) behind the palace. One other group of about a hundred men filled sandbags and placed them around the hooches.

Safety and security were the most important considerations in Baghdad. The thousands and thousands of sandbags surrounding the hooches ensured that rockets or mortars impacting the living area would only damage the area directly around the impact site. The walls of sandbags created a type of rocket "Russian Roulette." In other words, if a mortar landed within the sandbagged area of my hooch, I was toast! If it landed nearby, but outside the sandbagged area, I would survive. Late at night when it was still, it was sometimes possible to hear the faint *pop-pop* of mortars being fired from across the Tigris River toward the Green Zone. A few seconds later an explosion would be heard somewhere not too far away. The thought that runs through one's mind on evenings such as these is, "The odds of getting hit are very slim. The Green Zone is so big, and my sandbagged hooch is very small. Don't worry!"

I remember walking out the rear doors of the palace near my office one afternoon. I had taken one step outside the door and heard the sound of something above me. I looked up and saw a rocket racing parallel to the back of the palace forty or fifty feet in the air. I stepped back inside the safety of the palace, waited a few moments for the explosion, and then reexited.

On Easter Sunday of 2004, CH (MAJ) Lyn Brown and I were going to conduct a sunrise service. I went over to my office at 0500 hours to finalize the last few details for the service prior to sunrise. I'd only been in my office a few minutes when a huge explosion occurred about fifty meters from me. The first thought that shot through my mind was, "So, this is the sound of the stone door being blown off the tomb." That morning the Easter sunrise service was about half an hour after sunrise; the entire compound was in "lock down" mode for security purposes following the explosion.

The crew filling the sandbags worked all day long. Tens of thousands of sandbags created a beehive effect throughout the containerized living area. Walls of sandbags ten feet high and four feet wide at the base separated every hooch from every other hooch behind the palace. It was discovered, however, that there was one drawback. All the sandbags used for building the walls were biodegradable. The sun's rays would make quick work of them. Brilliant! Hours, literally hours, were spent discussing how to preserve the walls of sandbags at staff meetings.

✢

The United Nations compound in Baghdad had what one might describe as lax security. I believe that their security posture was intentional. I believe that the U.N. wanted to create a sense of solidarity with the Iraqi people. They didn't want to be enclosed within an enclave that made it difficult for Iraqis to access. The decision to sacrifice security for ease of access proved to be fatal when a truck bomb detonated, killing a host of U.N. employees and the senior U.N. official in Iraq, Mr. Sergio de Mello.

I am convinced that the bombing of the U.N. headquarters occurred for two primary reasons. First, it was an easy target of opportunity for the bombers. Second, the U.N. senior leadership was mistaken about the way in which the United Nations is perceived in much of the Arab world. We Westerners see the U.N. as a benevolent institution conducting humanitarian operations throughout the world. When Iraqis think of the United Nations, they think of the U.N. embargo. The suffering experienced by the Iraqi people following Operation Desert Storm was because the nations of the world placed an embargo on Iraq.

✢

Georges Sada had a relative serving on the Governing Council. The Governing Council was the Iraqi legislature working with the Coalition Provisional Authority. Georges's relative—I don't recall if he was a cousin, nephew, or uncle—lived in a walled compound with the other members of the Governing Council a few miles outside the Green Zone. I was invited to have dinner with Georges and the gentleman who served on the Governing Council one evening. I do not remember what we discussed that evening, although it was about politics and the future of Iraq. I don't remember what we had for dinner that evening, although I do remember it was a wonderful meal. What I remember is how tight the security was at the compound where the Governing Council members lived. There was a very high wall around the entire area, with tight security at the entrance. The inside of the compound was like a series of castles. Another wall surrounded each home. Private security guards from the families of the Council members protected each of these "castles." The most important necessity in Baghdad was having good security.

✢

It is a necessity that chaplains in a combat zone develop and rehearse a MASCAL SOP (mass casualty standing operating procedures). The MASCAL SOP will provide guidance for the duties of chaplains and chaplain assistants in the event of mass casualties. It is also essential that the MASCAL SOP be developed in coordination with medical personnel. The MASCAL SOP for the Coalition Provisional Authority directed that the CPA chapel be used as a hospital ward for overflow patients from the 28th CSH (combat support hospital—pronounced *cash*). It further directed that one chaplain would work in conjunction with the triage team and another would provide pastoral care to the patients in the chapel.

The day that the United Nations compound was truck bombed, I received a phone call from Colonel Dennis Sabal, CPA Chief of Staff, instructing me to exercise the MASCAL SOP. Two hours later the entire chapel had been turned into a 175-bed hospital ward. Dozens of individuals helped convert our worship and prayer area into a medical facility. It was as if members of one's family had been injured. Everyone pitched in to help. The chapel, it turned out, was not needed. The 28th CSH was able to handle all of the wounded.

✢

The evening that I bumped into Hamid al-Sharifi at the hotel in Kuwait City, something struck me about his appearance and mannerisms. I noticed that his left arm and hand hung limp at his side. More than once Hamid used his right hand to rub the fingers of his left hand and bend them back at the wrist. The first thing that occurred to me is that he must be recovering from a stoke that had paralyzed the left side of his body.

I asked, "Hamid, what happened to you? Did you have a stroke?"

"No," he replied. "Terrorists have attempted to kill me three different times. The last time I was attacked I was wounded in my arm and have suffered nerve damage. I keep moving my hand and arm to see if I can regain their use."

I don't believe that I lived in great fear during my year in Baghdad or experienced overwhelming trauma. I don't believe that I was psychologically damaged. I do believe, however, that I experienced continuous low-grade stress that impacted my thinking in Iraq and after I returned home.

The palace infrastructure was not sophisticated enough to handle the requirements placed upon it by the CPA. One of many problems in the palace was plumbing. The sewer was backing up and overflowing into the basement from time to time. To resolve this problem an Iraqi civilian contractor was hired to suck out the sewers beneath the palace on a daily basis. I placed myself in the terrorists' shoes. If I wanted to kill people working for the CPA, I would place a bomb in the large holding tank behind the cab of the truck. No one, absolutely no one, would open that tank up and look to see if a bomb had been placed inside. I must admit that every time I passed one of these trucks I wondered if it was going to explode and kill all of us. What an ignominious way to go!

Upon my return to CONUS (the continental United States), I was headed to breakfast and pulled into an IHOP parking lot. Someone had placed a coffee cup on the ground near the white line separating the spaces. My immediate thought: "Don't run over it, it'll explode; it's an IED." On the Fourth of July following my year in Baghdad, some kids were lighting firecrackers. The first string of them sounded like a semiautomatic rifle. I thought, "This is a wood frame room, bullets can come right through the walls. Where do I take cover if necessary?" Then I said to myself, "Dummy, you're back in the U.S., it's the Fourth of July, no one's shooting at you!"

The Iraqi day workers who cleaned the palace and built the sandbag walls surrounding the containerized living quarters were a friendly and outgoing group. Every time I passed them, I greeted them in Arabic. My rudimentary Arabic permitted me to say hello to them and ask how they were doing. I could ask their names and where they lived.

One day at lunchtime some of the individuals in the sandbag crew invited me to share their lunch with them. The typical lunch for the day workers was falafel. I enjoy Arab food, and I like falafel well enough, but didn't share lunch with them. It didn't seem right for me to take what little they had when I had so much. I did thank them very much for their offer and kindness.

It was at that very instant that something dawned on me. I was illiterate! I had never perceived of myself as an illiterate person, but in the Arab world that was exactly what I was. I could converse . . . a bit. I couldn't, however, read or write one letter in the Arabic alphabet. I needed to become literate. The very least I could do was learn to write my name in Arabic. It also dawned on me that I ought to learn how to write "Allah" in Arabic. I was a chaplain, after all.

My learning to write my name and "Allah" in Arabic took me a long way toward developing good relations with the Iraqi day workers. A couple of them invited me to visit them at their homes in the city. It was an invitation I could not accept. It was far too dangerous to travel into Baghdad and socialize with the day workers.

The grounds behind the palace and leading down to the Tigris River were packed with containerized living compartments, sandbags, and one other thing: signs! Americans love signs. We had signs for everything everywhere! KBR (Kellogg, Brown, and Root) had one employee who spent all his days making signs. Over time he acquired the name Sign Man. The signs he made were actually handsome. It was evident that he was a talented craftsman. He made large signs for the various containerized living areas with cut-out palm trees and raised lettering. I remember that the living area near the swimming pool was entitled Poolside Villas. We were living in tin boxes with a small window or two and a door. I don't exactly remember the name of my containerized living area. It was probably something like Tigris River Estates. What a hoot!

My favorite signs, however, were the little ones pounded into the ground just off the walkways behind the palace and informing everyone to "keep off the grass." The grass! What grass? There was no grass. There were a few weeds peeking up through the desert sand, but that was the extent of it. I came up with the idea for a sign but left Baghdad before I could ask Sign Man to make it for me. I was going to put it on the wall in the pool area. It was going to read, "No walking on the water! —CPA Chaplain."

The remains of United Nations' envoy Sergio de Mello were to be handed over to the Brazilian authorities in a ceremony at BIAP (Baghdad International Airport). Ambassador Bremer was to be present along with dignitaries from the U.N., the CPA, and the Brazilian government. I was requested to provide an invocation for the ceremony and at the appropriate time follow the casket carried by the honor guard to the plane. To ensure that the ceremony went exactly as planned, everyone involved, excluding the dignitaries, rehearsed for two hours proceeding the event. Those two hours were the hottest two hours of my year in Iraq. Actually, they were the hottest two hours of my life. The temperature on the tarmac was one hundred and fifty-six degrees Fahrenheit. The tar underfoot was bubbling up around the soles of our boots. My feet were baking.

It was a treat and an honor to bump into Hamid al-Sharifi in Kuwait City and have the opportunity to get to know him better during my year in the Kuwaiti desert. I visited him on two occasions at the Iraqi Embassy in Kuwait City, and he visited Camp Arifjan on two occasions. The second time he visited our base, he spoke to the senior leaders and gave his perspective on Iraqi-American relations, the state of affairs in Iraq, and his role as ambassador.

The thing that most impressed me about my friend Hamid is his great love for his country. He has such a strong devotion to Iraq and its people that nothing could prevent him from serving them.

Chapter 24

Chaplain (Lieutenant) Stephen Duesenberry

U.S. Navy

A young female M.P. spotted me outside the dining facility in the palace in Baghdad. Her rank was SPC4 (Specialist Fourth Class), and she appeared to be in her early twenties. "Chaplain, may I speak with you?"

"Certainly," I responded.

"Can I trust you?" she asked. "If I tell you things does that stay between you and me or will you talk to my chain of command?"

"What you say to me stays with me unless you intend to harm yourself or someone else," I explained. One of the primary responsibilities of the Chaplain Corps in the Army is suicide mitigation and prevention. If soldiers intend to harm themselves, it is a confidence a chaplain cannot keep.

"Is there someplace we can talk?" she asked. "I've been having this reoccurring nightmare and I need to talk to someone about it."

"Sure," I said, "come on down to my office right now, it's just around the corner."

I was introduced to Fritz Pearls, the father of Gestalt psychology, in seminary. I remember watching a film of him assisting a client in interpreting a dream. It was the most enlightening insight into the meaning of dreams that I have ever witnessed. Whenever someone wants to talk to me about dreams, I attempt lead that person along the path that Fritz Pearls revealed in the film with his client.

✠

TMEP is an acronym for Theater Mortuary Evacuation Point. It is located on the military side of the Kuwait City International Airport in an area controlled by the U.S. military. The TMEP is the facility that receives human remains from the theater of operations and prepares the remains for movement to CONUS (the continental United States). A Navy chaplain and Marine gunnery sergeant assigned to support the chaplain provide religious support at the TMEP. Because I served as the command chaplain for the 377th Theater Support Command that controls the movement of supplies and personnel in and out of theater, the chaplain and gunnery sergeant reported to me.

Furthermore, I was responsible for writing the SOPs (standing operating procedures) for ramp ceremonies during "uploads." The TMEP SOP was a twelve page document that carefully established the honors to be rendered for human remains as they were loaded onto aircraft for transfer to Germany and then on to Dover Air Force Base (A.F.B.) in Dover, Delaware. The TMEP SOP also established guidance for the TMEP chaplain in providing prayers during the upload ceremony. The transport of human remains from the theater of operations to CONUS does not employ the use of a coffin. Transfer cases are used for the movement of human remains. These cases are made of metal and are large enough to permit bags of ice to be placed in certain positions under and above the body for movement. Transfer cases containing human remains and ice weigh about four hundred pounds. From the moment the transfer case(s) leaves the TMEP facility until the moment it is secured in the cargo area of the aircraft, every word spoken by the chaplain and every action by those rendering honors is carefully scripted.

Life in the desert is generally miserable. It is either extremely hot or extremely cold. It is a place of extremes. When I was in Baghdad, I often wondered if the extremes of desert life are what contribute to the extreme responses some Arabs make to seemingly insignificant events. I don't believe that it is an accident that much of the anarchy in the history of Iraq happened in the miserable heat of summer. The bridge across the Tigris River near the former presidential palace is called the Fourteenth of July Bridge in remembrance of the Baathist overthrow of the government on that date.

I shared a bedroom on the second floor of the palace with seven of my "best new friends" for about two months following our arrival in Baghdad. The room was devoid of furniture except for the brand-new beds that had been purchased for us. Duffel bags littered the floor and makeshift tables served as nightstands. The most prominent feature of the room was a large crystal chandelier in the center of the ceiling. During the month of May, the room was cool enough for sleeping comfortably at night with the window open. Of course, the sound of constant gunfire did tend to wake one up at times. Also, the sound of tracks (tanks and armored personnel carriers) on the streets outside the palace made it sound as if one were living adjacent to the railroad. As the cool nights of May turned to the stinking hot nights of June, all of my roommates and I were issued floor fans to keep the air moving around our beds. Each one of us had a fan, and each fan was located at the foot of our beds. We soon discovered, however, that fans moving hot air around the room felt more like hair dryers aimed at us than a useful method for cooling off. Three or four times each night I would wake up soaking wet from sweat, move my pillow to the other end of the bed so I wasn't sleeping in a pool, and try to go back to sleep.

✢

The female M.P. followed me around the corner to my office. The office was actually just a dead end elbow at the end of the hallway that ran parallel to the back of the palace. Months earlier I had been informed that I would have to move my office location. It was recommended that I move upstairs. It was hot enough downstairs in the heat of the day, and I couldn't imagine trying to work where it was hotter still. I had scouted the palace and found this space. No one particularly cared about the space because it was "just a hallway." KBR (Kellogg, Brown, and Root) construction workers built a wall and doorway to provide privacy.

It turned out to be the best office in the entire building. It was spacious. I ended up furnishing the space with furniture from Uday's house a few blocks away. The furniture was absolutely gaudy, but it was made for a room with marble floors, walls, and ornate chandelier. I had room for a sitting area with sofa, coffee table, and end tables and chairs. There was room for three workstations and a large mahogany table seating ten. And I had bookshelves, display cases with knickknacks, and oriental rugs. I also had a welcome area with a fancy chair and a small round table where I displayed Bibles in English, Spanish, and Arabic along with Qur'ans. They were there for the taking. Hey, what's the point of going to war if one can't improve one's "foxhole"?

We sat down and the specialist began to tell me her dream. She was in a dance hall somewhere. It was a very large place with a bar off to one side. Above the dance floor was one of those globes with the many-faceted mirrors covering it and creating the sensation of little lights dancing on the floor. Off in the corner was a strobe light, and its intermittent beams made the entire place surreal. Everyone appeared to be moving in slow motion. She was dancing with her father. As they danced, her father grabbed his chest and fell to the floor in agony. It was evident that he was having a heart attack. She watched in a panic unable to help him. He died right before her eyes.

She'd been having this dream for about three weeks' time. What did it mean?

Chaplain (LT) Stephen Duesenberry, U.S.N., an Orthodox priest, was the TMEP chaplain when I arrived in Kuwait. Shortly after our arrival in Kuwait, I was given a tour of the TMEP facility and was briefed on their mission. A team of mortuary affairs personnel inventories everything on the remains when they arrive in Kuwait. The remains arrive from theater with everything that was present when the individual died . . . flak jackets, uniforms, boots, etc. The mortuary affairs personnel carefully remove items from pockets and watches from wrists. Each item is recorded, and personal effects are placed in a plastic bag that accompanies the remains. As the body bags were open, CH Duesenberry's responsibility was to stand at the foot of each gurney and pray for the repose of the soul of each set of remains. He would then make an annotation on each death certificate that prayers had been offered for this individual.

The TMEP chaplain also provided pastoral care and counseling for the mortuary affairs team during periods of quiet between downloads and uploads (i.e., the arrival and departure of human remains). This was especially important when remains were received that had been abused or tortured by terrorists. I though that I had been on holy ground during my deployment to Iraq. But here at TMEP I was in the most sacred space I will ever see in my life. It was all I could do not to begin weeping each time I entered the building. I couldn't comprehend how in the world CH Duesenberry had the stamina to do his job. I determined at that moment that one of my primary responsibilities as the command chaplain and his supervisor would be to pray for him by name daily. The TMEP chaplain is a six-month rotation, not a yearlong deployment, for obvious reasons. The same thing is true for mortuary affairs personnel. The mortuary affairs personnel also work in shifts that give them a few days off in between their time at TMEP. Three Navy chaplains and Marine gunnery sergeants were assigned to serve at the TMEP during my tenure as 377th TSC Command Chaplain.

The worst thing about desert life, in my opinion, is sandstorms. Sandstorms are to be expected during the month of June and July. The air is filled with dust and particles of sand. The problem isn't so much that it fills the air and gets into one's clothing and lungs. The problem is that it assaults the eyes. The military does issue wraparound sunglasses to personnel to provide protection from dust and debris. They are effective . . . most of the time! One is constantly trying to get the sand out of one's eyes and mouth. Who needs whitening strips for teeth when the abrasive affect of blowing dirt will brighten one's smile?

During occasions of intense wind, the sky turns brown. It almost looks like a gray New England snowy day except for the color of the sky. Because the sky is so dark and visibility limited, U.S. military convoys are restricted from travel. This is also true of any other coalition personnel. On more than one occasion, CH (LT) John Carter, the third TMEP chaplain during my tour in Kuwait, had to receive special permission to return to the airbase for the download of human remains.

I remember having a conversation one afternoon in Iraq with a number of soldiers who were trying to capture the essence of living in the desert to share with family members and friends back home. This is what they finally came up with. Wait until the hottest day of the summer. Then, turn the heat as high as possible. Go into the kitchen and turn on the oven. Sit right in front of the open oven door wearing everything you own!

When they finished this amusing exchange, I said, "You've forgotten one thing. They've got to get their vacuum cleaners and reverse the motor so it blows all the dust it has collected into the air. It must shower down on them and stick to their faces and get in their eyes and mouth." *That* is desert living!

✝

The M.P. had finished telling me her dream, so I asked her to do something for me. I wanted her to reenter the dream and tell it to me again. This time, however, I did not want her to be herself, I wanted her to be the many-faceted mirror globe hanging from the ceiling.

The essence of Gestalt dream interpretation I'd witnessed from the Fritz Pearls film was investigating the dream from different perspectives. Fritz would have his clients become some other part of the dream and then speak about it in the first person. It didn't take long for me to realize that having the M.P. assume the perspective of the globe wasn't going to work. I then requested that she see herself as the strobe light in the corner. She began.

"I am a strobe light and I am bolted to a wall in the corner of a dance hall. Beneath me is a large dance floor, and there are quite a few couples dancing to the music. There is a bar in this dance hall beyond the dance floor. There are also tables and chairs throughout the building. I am a bright light, and the effect I create with my strobe is that everything is happening in slow motion. I look down at the dance floor and I see couples dancing. They look like they're in a silent movie. As I watch the couples dance, I see one couple that appears curious. He is much older than she is, but it appears that they know each other and are having a good time. Suddenly the man grabs his chest and falls to the floor. His dance partner is terror stricken and can't do a thing. I can see that he is having a heart attack, but I am stuck up here in the corner and am helpless to do anything."

I said to her, "Say that again."

"I am stuck up here in the corner and am helpless to do anything."

I said, "Say that again."

She said, "I am stuck up here. . . . " Then she stopped.

"You know," she said, "I go out on patrol and on convoy escort every day. I ride shotgun in one of our vehicles. From time to time we pull over on the side of the roads to take a break and to check the vehicles. Whenever we do this Iraqi children seem to come out of nowhere and gather around our vehicles. These kids don't have anything, and we have so much. I always reach into the HUMMER and get some candy from my MREs ("meals ready to eat"—military rations) to give to them. If I don't have candy, I'll give them something else from my MRE or some bottled water. My staff sergeant has been telling me that it is against policy to give anything to the Iraqi children. But I just can't help myself. I see these poor children, and my heart goes out to them. I have to do something.

"About three weeks ago, my staff sergeant moved me out of the shotgun position and put me up in the copula manning the machine gun. When we pulled off the road for a break, the children gathered around the vehicles, but I was stuck up in the copula and was helpless to do anything. I wanted to give them something. My heart was aching for them, but I was stuck in the copula and helpless. Just after that the reoccurring dream began."

This soldier's dream wasn't about her father having a heart attack and dying while dancing with her. The dream was about her inability to render aid to young Iraqi children who had so little while she had so much to give.

Human remains are received at TMEP around the clock as planes come in from Iraq. Human remains are also uploaded at any time of the day or night when planes depart for Germany. The upload ceremony is a solemn and dignified military ceremony in which military honors are rendered and prayers said over our fallen comrades. Each transfer case is removed from a transport vehicle and placed onboard the plane or on an elevator that lifts it up to the plane's cargo hold. As the flag-draped transfer cases are moved by pallbearers, a four-second salute (saluting in such a manner as to require four seconds in bringing one's hand to one's face) is rendered by those in formation beside the plane. My commanding general in Kuwait insisted on attending the upload ceremonies for all personnel in his command who were killed in action during our deployment (he lost five soldiers during his year of command killed by IEDs). The upload ceremonies for personnel from our command all occurred between 0200 hours and 0400 hours. We left Camp Arifjan at about midnight in order not to miss the ceremonies because military planes do not necessarily leave according to schedule, but according to mission requirements.

The human remains of U.S. military personnel are flown from Kuwait to Germany. In Germany, the transfer cases are opened, and the bags of ice are replaced with new bags of ice. Military honors are rendered each time the flag-draped transfer cases are downloaded or uploaded. The remains are then transported to Dover Air Force Base, Delaware. A general officer in the U.S. military is present at Dover to greet each and every plane that lands with human remains. The remains are then taken to the morgue. When the work at the morgue is completed, the remains are placed in a coffin. The remains are placed in a dress uniform from the deceased's branch of service. In the event that the remains cannot be placed in a uniform, the uniform is draped over the body. A wall in the building where the remains are dressed contains all the military decorations to which one might be entitled. These decorations are placed in their proper order on the uniform. Every detail about the uniform is inspected. Every crease in the uniform is inspected, and every piece of lint or bit of thread is removed. The coffin is then draped with an American flag, and the remains are ready to be returned to the family.

The upload and download of the remains of U.S. military personnel is not open to the public or press. It is not a spectacle to be gawked at. It is a solemn event requiring the utmost dignity.

✠

It is impossible to serve in Iraq and to supervise chaplains who carry out their sacred duties at TMEP and not ask very important questions. These questions include, Is it worth it? Is our presence in Iraq, our Global War on Terrorism, worth the price?

I can only answer these questions for myself. I cannot answer for a mother who has just lost her eighteen-year-old son to a roadside bomb. I cannot answer for the mother of three small children who has just lost her husband to a rocket attack. I cannot answer for a child who has just lost Mommy in a suicide car bomb in Baghdad. I can, however, answer for myself.

Like the M.P. whose heart continually went out to the children of Iraq, I know Iraq as much more than a place on a map or debate in our body politic.

Iraq is my friend Maher and his wife Mona. Iraq is May Hanna and Farias. Iraq is Hamid al-Sharifi and Sheikh Fuad Rashid. Iraq is Fatima and Ibrahim. Iraq is Nahla and Hadeel. It is Georges Sada and interim Prime Minister Allawi. Iraq is a hundred thousand souls crying out from mass graves for justice and for peace.

If I had died in Iraq, if I had lost my life helping my friends build a nation where they could live in peace and free from the fear of murder and rape at the hands of their own leaders, it would have been well worth the sacrifice. It would have been an honor. I do not have a death wish, and I do not particularly like the idea of the pain associated with dying, especially getting blown up by an IED, car bomb, or rocket. But I can think of no greater privilege than to give my life for my friends. I can think of nothing better than giving my life for something that enhances the quality of life and respect for human dignity that will become the new life story of Iraq.

Chapter 25

Major General Thomas Robinson

U.S. Army Reserve

The United States honors those who have given their lives in the service of our country on a number of occasions each year. We remember our war dead on Veteran's Day, Memorial Day, and the Fourth of July. The Army also remembers its fallen on the Army birthday and at events such as a dining-in. We inevitably hear speeches on these occasions that extol the virtues of those who "made the ultimate sacrifice" or "paid the ultimate price." The keynote speakers on these occasions, while well-intentioned and well-meaning, completely miss the mark in my opinion.

The fact of the matter is that those who died in the service of our country did not pay the ultimate price. Death is not the ultimate sacrifice, is it? Those who have died in the service of our country may have considered the loss of our freedoms a more precious sacrifice than the loss of their own lives. The ultimate price for some who have sacrificed their lives in service to our country may have been the death of a "battle buddy." There are literally hundreds or thousands of things that individuals consider the ultimate sacrifice and for which they are willing to give their lives as the lesser of two values. Some of these things reflect our highest ideals and noblest aspirations. Some of them are much more pragmatic in nature, like getting enough money to go to college. Whatever the case is, one thing is certain: those who have died in the service of our country have not paid the ultimate price!

✠

I am a retired colonel and Army chaplain. I served in the Army more than twenty-five years. Yet in all my years in the military and attaining the senior field grade rank, I have never been to the Pentagon in the performance of my duties. I have worked with hundreds of Pentagon officials and have even been invited to tour the Pentagon on occasion, but have never visited it in my capacity as an

Army officer. I did go to the Pentagon on one occasion, however. It was in 1972, and it was to participate in a "Mass for peace" as part of an antiwar protest during the Vietnam War. This service was conducted in one of the concourses within the building. My Army friends are entertained by this fact about my military career.

Today's Army and military is an all-volunteer force. The all-volunteer force is extolled as a quasi-virtue within the United States both by the military and the civilian sector as well. I see it differently. What the all-volunteer force perpetuates is military personnel who do what they are told when they are told to do it. "You volunteered to be here, now do what you're told!" Of course, these exact words are not generally spoken, but they are always implied.

The World War II and Cold War eras filled the ranks of the military through the draft. What the draft guaranteed was a fairly well-trained force that asked questions. Soldiers who were just out of college wanted to know why they were being ordered to do certain things. Soldiers who were serving a required enlistment of two years questioned the authority and decisions of their superiors. The all-volunteer military doesn't ask questions. It doesn't question authority. "You're here because you chose to be here. Now, shut up and do what you've been told to do. Don't like it? Then why'd you join in the first place? Who cares that you've been deployed for four or five years since 9/11? You chose this life; no one made you do it. If you don't like it, get out!" The Army mantra is, "When we want your opinion, we'll give it to you!" No wonder we have general officers who speak out against the war in Iraq after their military career is over. They were never truly permitted to speak their minds when they served.

✢

I believe that most competent historians will disagree with what I am about to say. They will probably suggest that my conclusions are naïve and much too simplistic. They are probably right. Nevertheless, here goes.

What caused the decline and fall of the Roman Empire? I am convinced that it was the fact that Roman citizens had stopped, for the most part, serving in the Roman army. The Roman Empire had gotten to the point where mercenaries defended it. Roman citizens who were the beneficiaries of the abundance of Rome were unwilling to place their lives in jeopardy for the greater good of the empire. For them, death was the ultimate sacrifice. The mercenaries who defended Rome discovered that someone else's "stuff" was not worth dying for. For them, death was the ultimate price to be paid. When the going got tough, they got going!

✢

MG Thomas D. Robinson was my commanding general (CG) during the year in which I was deployed to Kuwait. It was the CG's custom to hold a social for the members of his command each month. We would generally gather at a pavilion on Camp Arifjan for these events. We would have something to eat, welcome incoming personnel, and say farewell to those departing. On one occasion, the CG decided to give certificates to those within the command who had served in the Army more than thirty years. The certificate had been framed, and it was a lovely keepsake for those who received them.

As the certificates were read and the individuals came forward to receive them, I was shocked at how many names were called. I had expected that a handful of people would be recognized, maybe a dozen at most. It was unfathomable to me that more than forty people within the command received certificates. I was aware that I was serving in a senior reserve command and that senior reserve commands are populated with older individuals, but this was shocking to me.

A thought ran through my mind: "This is your grandfather's war, and guess what? Granddad and grandma are here fighting it!" Another thought shot through my mind: "Where are the young men of America?" It wasn't a question with a hidden agenda, like, if the old folks have to be here, why aren't the young and strong also present? Those with whom I was deployed in Kuwait were happy to be serving their country.

I glanced around at the others who were attending the CG's social. Many of them were women. The thought ran through my mind again: "Where are the young men of America?" I didn't say this to myself because I don't believe that women ought to be soldiers or that they are not very good at what they do. The women in today's military are extremely intelligent and competent warriors. But where, I wondered, were the young men of our country?

Monthly in Kuwait or Iraq, it seemed to me, one hundred or more U.S. soldiers gather for an impressive ceremony in which they became citizens of the United States. We have literally hundreds and hundreds of soldiers from foreign countries serving in our armed forces. And the thought runs through my mind: "Where are the young men of America?" I would hazard a guess that 15 percent of today's U.S. Army is composed of grandparents (or people the age of grandparents), women, and foreigners. I am not an alarmist and do not have a tendency to overreact, but I find this fact alarming.

✝

Prior to being accessioned into the Army as a chaplain in 1982, I was required to sign a waiver. That waiver stated that because I had passed my thirty-fifth birthday, I was not entitled to and did not expect a pension from the military at the time of my release. The reason that I was required to sign the waiver is that the normal retirement age for military personnel in 1982 was fifty-five years of age. Since I could not achieve twenty years of service before my mandatory retirement date, I needed to acknowledge the fact that I might not be entitled to a military pension.

I returned from Kuwait and was sent to Ft. Bliss, Texas, to complete the demobilization process. One afternoon I hopped on the shuttle bus and traveled to the PX to pick up a few items. I had finished shopping and upon my return to the bus stop encountered a dozen AIT (advanced individual training) students. AIT immediately follows basic training for enlisted personnel and educates them to perform their MOS (military occupational specialty). Since they were much lower ranking soldiers and relatively new to the Army, they snapped to attention and saluted me. I returned the salute and engaged them in conversation. I asked them about their MOSs and how they were doing. I asked them about their next assignments and how their families back home were coping with their decision to join the Army.

In the course of our conversation, I learned that one of these AIT students was forty-two years old. I was shocked. How in the world did this fellow get into the Army at his age? The last I knew, one had to be in one's twenties to enlist in the Army.

The Army, along with the Navy, Marine Corps, and Air Force, publishes its monthly recruiting figures. The recent recruiting figures make it appear as if all the services are meeting their recruiting requirements. Figures can be deceiving, however.

The Army has raised the entrance age of its recruits because it cannot draw in enough personnel from the manpower base of younger men and women in order to meet its recruiting objectives. Soldiers who reenlist are being given large bonuses. The typical bonus for junior enlisted soldiers is $15,000 for a six-year extension. Soldiers who reenlist within the combat theater of operations receive their bonus tax free. No wonder it appears as if everyone who serves the Army in Iraq, Afghanistan, and Kuwait wants to stay in the military.

The fact of the matter is that the Army recruiting goals are so difficult to achieve that the Army is now paying its own soldiers two thousand dollars apiece for each new recruit that they bring in and who completes his or her initial training. The soldiers of the Army Reserve command in which I served prior to my retirement were all required to register as subcontractors for a civilian company that manages Army Reserve recruiting. I think it is shocking that new recruits to the Army can be as old as forty-two years of age. That means that they will retire from Army at sixty-two. Recently the Chief of Army Chaplains followed these new recruiting guidelines by increasing the age of chaplain accessions to forty-seven years of age. The Chief of Army Chaplains may authorize the extension of chaplains to the age of sixty-seven. I find it shocking that this is required in order to fill vacant chaplain billets. We jokingly say that if the chaplain is a Roman Catholic priest he may stay until he dies of old age! I met one Roman Catholic priest who expected to remain in the Army until the age of seventy.

The Army is experiencing an unprecedented "graying of the force." This is now a Reserve phenomenon but will also be experienced in the Active Component as forty-two-year-old recruits reach the midcareer point.

Atop Saddam's former presidential palace in Baghdad were four huge busts of the dictator. Each of these was twenty-four feet high. These busts were so prominent that the palace became known as the "four head palace."

The young service men and women who visited the palace, however, gave the place a different nickname. They observed us "old folks" with gray and thinning hair working for the Coalition Provisional Authority and dubbed it the "forehead palace"! I must admit that I love American service men and women because they are intellectually sharp and very, very quick. U.S. service members living in the most difficult of circumstances under the most hazardous conditions somehow always manage to find the humor in it. When I was deployed to Bosnia in 1998, I shared a hooch with LTC Ron Taylor. It didn't take long before someone at Eagle Base made the connection between Ron and me, the chaplain, sharing living quarters. A stenciled nameplate quickly appeared beside our front door. It read: "Lord and Taylor."

I mobilized at Ft. Benning, Georgia, for my tour in Iraq. The total number of people being mobilized during the week I was at the MOB station exceeded four hundred military and civilian personnel. A number of the individuals being mobilized had been involuntary recalls to active duty. What that means is that these individuals had spent years in the military, retired and were receiving Army pensions and then were recalled to active duty. I met a group of four or five individuals who each had twenty or more years of Army service and who had been working in the civilian sector. The Army had reached out and gobbled them up. Moreover, these fellows had been sent back to basic training for a refresher before arriving at the MOB station! Yikes! Basic training is a challenge for young men and women. Imagine what it must have been like for this group in their late forties and early fifties.

The Army has been doing everything possible to fill its ranks. It has raised the age of enlistment. It is offering large bonuses for enlistment and for reenlistment. It has made every soldier a recruiter by offering two thousand dollars for each individual brought in. And the Army is pulling civilians out of retirement involuntarily. What is going to happen when we run out of forty-two-year-olds? Will we begin lowering the age for service? We already permit high school juniors to attend basic training during the summer before their senior year. They can then complete their AIT immediately upon graduation.

✢

I spent sixteen months on active duty with the military between my tours in Iraq and Kuwait at Ft. Devens, Massachusetts. Each day at lunchtime a group of us would go out to any one of a number of restaurants and diners in the area. One cold February day at lunch with my friends I looked out the window and spotted an elderly couple trying to get out of their car and make their way into the diner. The wife had driven her feeble husband to lunch and had walked around to the passenger side of the car to help him get out. It was a very windy day, and the wind was forcing the passenger door closed on them both. He had a cane and was trying to get to his feet out of the car and on the ice-covered ground. She was tugging on his sleeve to help him stand. I watched them struggle for a few moments and it was evident to me that they'd be stuck for hours trying to make their way into the diner.

I got up from my meal, put on my field jacket and beret, and went outside to assist them. I got the old fellow out of the car and over a mound of ice and snow to the sidewalk. I escorted him into the diner and sat him at the table closest to the door. I then went back to my table and finished lunch with my friends. When it came time for us to pay at the cash register and leave, I was not permitted to pay. The owner of the diner had watched what I had done and was so moved by my action that my lunch was free.

I do not share this vignette in order to drawing attention to myself. Nor do I share this as way of letting one know what a great humanitarian I am. My response to the couple attempting to enter the diner was really not a big deal. It was merely a simple act of kindness that required very little effort on my part. I share this story because while it was something I surely would have forgotten later that day, it was an uncommon sight for the restaurant owner. For her, my actions were extraordinary. How is it possible that simple courtesy in our society has now been raised to the level of the extraordinary?

The truth of the matter is that the "crisis" (my word, not the Army spin) in recruiting is a microcosm of our society in general. The era of President Kennedy's "Ask not what your country can do for you, but what you can do for your country" is past. Service, whether in the military or at the local diner, seems not to be the rule but the exception.

Serving in the U.S. military means defending the rights of those who may hold diametrically opposing views to one's own. In other words, military personnel will fight and die in order to preserve the right of other Americans to tell them that they are stupid for serving their country. This is the American way. Our liberties are not just for those who think and act the way we do. But perhaps the time has come to question the integrity of the dialogue between individuals who hold diametrically opposing views. Is it enough to merely "talk the talk" and not "walk the walk"? Or, to put it into my own words and not the cliché of the recovery community, we've got to bring more than just our appetites to the table! I am convinced that words spoken must be reinforced by actions. If not, then we need to question the veracity of what is said.

One of the responsibilities of Army chaplains is to interview soldiers who claim to be conscientious objectors and who desire to be released from the military. I have had occasion to interview a number of individuals seeking conscientious objector (CO) status and generally find them to be sincere in their beliefs. Prior to my deployment to Kuwait, however, I had the occasion to interview a captain in the Army Medical Corps.

This individual had received more than $184,000 in tuition assistance for medical education from the Army. Now that this individual was about to be mobilized with a medical unit and deployed she discovered that she was a conscientious objector. I completed the required interview and stated in my memorandum that I was not convinced that this individual was sincere in her beliefs. My conclusion, which, by the way, differed from both the command surgeon's office and the investigating JAG officer, swayed the review board, who denied CO status to this individual. A federal court, however, reversed the decision of the board and asserted that my conclusion was baseless.

I am not certain how the recruiting crisis in the U.S. Army is going to be resolved. Should we bring back the draft? Should we require compulsory service of some sort for all citizens, one option of which could be duty in the armed services? Or do we need to resolve this crisis at all? Isn't it enough that our citizens pay their taxes and vote on Election Day? Isn't it in our best interest to let those who want to serve serve? Is there really anything that citizens need to bring to the table besides their appetites? Are any of us really required to sacrifice anything in order for democracy to prosper?

Chapter 26

Chaplain (Colonel) Frank E. Wismer III

U.S. Army Reserve

I strive to live by a five-point rule of life. I have touched on number of these points while discussing my experiences as a soldier, chaplain, and Reservist mobilized in the Global War on Terrorism. My rule of life is not an objective standard that I have imposed or inflicted upon myself from without. It is the essence of who, with God's help, I have discovered myself to be within. The discovery and articulation of my rule has been the most significant revelation of my life. Living into the fullness of my rule has been the greatest challenge of my life.

The fifth point of my rule of life states, "I am no longer willing to cooperate with those who seek to diminish me or another." I added the final two words "or another" long after discovering the initial aspect of this fifth point in my rule. It is not enough for me merely to resist those who desire to strip away my dignity. I am compelled to resist those who would strip others of their dignity as well. And I must catch myself from the pitfall of saying or doing anything that would diminish the stature of another. I dare say that living out my rule of life on a daily basis is a continuous struggle. There are occasions when I allow others to diminish me. There are times when I stand idly by as others are belittled. There are still far too many occasions when I steal the dignity of another through careless or intentional insults and ridicule.

✠

The university I attended offered a course called Russian Literature in Translation. In it, we were introduced to the great Russian authors like Tolstoy, Pushkin, Dostoevsky, and Pasternak. What I particularly liked was their incredible insights into life and the theology that sprang from these insights. I still find Dostoevsky's chapter on the Grand Inquisitor in his book *The Brothers Karamazov* to be the primer for examining the temptation of Jesus in the wilderness prior to his public ministry.

The Gulag Archipelago, Aleksandr Solzhenitsyn's three-volume work, was published in 1973. My fascination with Russian authors compelled me to read the entire trilogy. Reading it was a laborious endeavor, but toward the end of his second volume Solzhenitsyn finally shares with the reader his profound theology. I am certain that I will not remember his words exactly, but I believe I've captured his intent. "I have finally discovered the truth about all the religions of the world. They do not attempt to expel evil from the world in its entirety, but to constrict it within each individual."

Less than a week following the events of September 11, 2001, we held a memorial service at the church I served in Worcester, Massachusetts. It was a simple service without prayers or hymns. There was no sermon and no public profession of faith. There were no worship leaders and there was no organist. Each individual who entered the church was presented with the names of those who had been killed and asked to sit in silence with their own thoughts for as long a time as they chose to do so. A CD provided appropriate music for contemplation and reflection in the background.

It was during this service as I sat in silence contemplating the names of those who had died that the rage I felt toward what had occurred less than a week earlier dissipated. It was replaced by a resolve not to allow myself to be terrorized. If it was the intent of the terrorists to terrorize our country, it seemed self-evident to me that it was the duty of every American to live without fear. Months before the Global War on Terrorism began, I initiated my own Personal War on Terrorism. Moreover, I was convinced that a fitting tribute or memorial to those who had been killed on September 11th was to be fearless.

I am fairly certain that my Personal War on Terrorism must have begun as an idea planted in my mind by something I heard on the television immediately following 9/11. It was during the memorial service, however, that I appropriated this thought as my personal mission in response to terrorism.

The Global War on Terrorism is a geopolitical confrontation between the United States–led coalition and an international religious-based (the term al Qaeda means "the base" or "the foundation") insurgency. The Personal War on Terrorism is an individual struggle not to succumb to fear or be held prisoner to the bondage of fear. It is one's personal exodus journey from captivity to freedom. It is a spiritual quest and the prototypical story of the Jewish and Christian scriptures. It is the spiritual essence of jihad. It is each individual's confrontation with his or her demons. It is a conscious decision to seek freedom from the domination of anger, anxiety, shame, rage, and retribution. It is an unwillingness to be dominated by one's own worries or the threats of another. It is the historical revelation of God being played out in God's people from generation to generation. It is a personal resolve, an unwillingness to cooperate with those who seek to diminish us as well as others. It is the truth of all the religions of the world.

Toward the end of my deployment to Kuwait, a soldier from one of our subordinate commands was killed by an IED while on convoy in Iraq. To memorialize this soldier, his unit held a ceremony at the chapel on Camp Arifjan. The chapel at Camp Arifjan was originally intended to serve as the base theater. It seats more than six hundred and fifty people. The chapel was filled to overflowing by the time I arrived, and many soldiers were already standing in the aisles on both sides of the theater. Thankfully, seats had been reserved for senior officers in the first three rows of the chapel, and I was escorted to a seat in the third row on the left-hand side of the auditorium. After I was seated, I began to look around to get a glimpse at who else was in attendance. The deputy Third Army commander was present, as were members of the Third Army staff. The soldier's entire battalion was present, at least those who were not out on convoy. There were soldiers present who were in the sister battalions of the soldier who had been killed. What seemed to be singularly lacking, in my opinion, was anyone else in the chapel from our command. It was our command that had published the FRAGO (fragmentary order) directing the mission on which this soldier had lost his life. The longer I sat waiting for the ceremony to begin, the angrier I became.

Thankfully, the ceremony began and helped to put me in the proper frame of mind. It was the epitome of what every memorial ceremony ought to be. It was excellently prepared and rehearsed. It was personal and caring. It made one leave the chapel wishing that he or she had been given the privilege of knowing that soldier. Following the ceremony, those present were invited to come forward and pay respects to their fallen comrade. There was a stand on which a picture of the soldier had been placed. A rifle was placed upside down in the stand with the bayonet securing it to the stand. The soldier's helmet rested on the stock end of the rifle, and dog tags dangled down. Beginning with the senior ranking officers present, individuals or groups of individuals stood in front of the display and saluted. They then presented a coin or token of their esteem, saluted again, and departed.

The memorial ceremony began at 1400 hours and lasted just about an hour. I knew that I had a staff meeting at 1500 hours and began getting a bit anxious that I'd be late because of all the individuals paying their respects. By the time I left the chapel, my staff meeting a mile away was just beginning. I quickly walked to our headquarters, all the while wondering who might make some offhanded comment about me being late. I was also getting myself loaded for bear. I was incredulous that no one else from our command appeared to be present, and I was girding myself for a snide remark about being late to the staff meeting. I walked into a packed conference room and found a place to sit. I was the last one to enter the room. Sure enough, it only took about three minutes until the chief of staff reamed out all of those who were late to staff meetings.

It was at that moment that I released the fury I'd built up within me prior to and following the memorial ceremony. I looked right at the chief and blurted, "Next time, Chief, I'll be certain to see that the memorial ceremony for one of our fallen soldiers doesn't interfere with this important meeting!" You could have heard a pin drop. Oh, baby! The staff didn't often see this side of me. Needless to say, the chief directed me to report to his office following the meeting for a perfunctory chewing out.

The next day, COL Mike Ford, our G-3 (individual responsible for plans and operations) and a West Point graduate, took me aside and chastised me for my words at the staff meeting. He said two things that I found very insightful. First, he informed me that a chief of staff needs to win all the public debates, especially among his peers. This is important if he is to have the respect of the junior officers. Second, he told me that he and all the staff looked to me to be the voice of calm and reason. I had to be the one constant in the midst of chaos.

I spent the rest of the day thinking about what Mike had said to me. There was no way around it; he was right on target. The chief of staff did need to win the public battles among his peers, and I needed to permit him to do that. I also had to remember to be the voice of calm in the midst of chaos. I went to see Mike and let him know that I got it and thanked him for the insight given me.

From the perspective of my rule of life, I'd gotten it half right. I did not allow myself to cooperate with someone I perceived wanted to diminish me. I did, however, diminish that person by my sharp tongue. "I have finally discovered the truth about all the religions of the world. They do not attempt to expel evil from the world in its entirety, but to constrict it within each individual."

Chaplain (Colonel) Frank E. Wismer III

I don't believe it is enough for the United States to win the Global War on Terrorism. We must also, as a people, win the Personal War on Terrorism. It isn't good enough for our soldiers to finally come home from Iraq and Afghanistan victorious in the global war if in the process they lose the personal war that strips away human dignity. It isn't enough if our nation defeats terrorism in the world if in the process we diminish those who hold and express opinions that differ from our own. It isn't enough to expel evil from the world in its entirety if we cannot constrict it within ourselves individually.

I was requested to provide a short prayer for a memorial ceremony outside the Coalition Provisional Authority headquarters on September 11, 2003. I prayed the following: "Let us attune our hearts to the voices crying out from September 11, 2001, compelling us to eradicate terrorism in our world and restore justice and dignity to all creation." Perhaps Aleksandr Solzhenitsyn is correct, and we never ever expel evil from the world in its entirety. We can, however, constrict it within ourselves.

Notes

Chapter 3

1. Meditation from Lenten Meditation Guide prepared by me in Kuwait 2007.

Chapter 13

1. Julia Goldman, "Chanukah at Saddam's Palace: Iraqi Jew's Menorah Heavy with Symbolism," *The Jewish Week,* December 19, 2003, http://findarticles.com/p/articles/mi_hb5092/is_200312/ai_n18523200 (accessed 13 January 2008).
2. Carol A. Valentine, "911 Lawsuit Is a Booby Trap," *Public Action*, 3 March 2004, http://www.public-action.com/911/suit.html (accessed 17 January 2008).

Chapter 14

1. "Yezidiism," *About.com: Alternative Religions*, http://altreligion.about.com/library/faqs/bl_yezidism.htm (accessed 23 January 2008).

Chapter 16

1. Hammurabi, "Hammurabi's Code of Laws," translated by L. W. King, Exploring Ancient World Cultures, University of Evansville, http://eawc.evansville.edu/anthology/hammurabi.htm (accessed January 2008).

Chapter 17

1. Wikipedia, s.v. "Philip Bloom," http://en.wikipedia.org/wiki/Philip_Bloom (accessed 6 November 2007).

Chapter 18

1. The Very Rev. John Breck, "The Gift of Silence," *Orthodox Church in America*, http://www.oca.org/CHRIST-life-print.asp?ID=76 (accessed 30 January 2008).

Chapter 20

1. Robert Collier, "Eccentric Ally in Green Zone," *San Franscisco Chronicle*, 31 July 2004, http://www.sfgate.com/cgi-bin/article.cgi?f=/c/a/2004/07/31/MNGDM80L0P1.DTL&hw=Eccentric+ally+in+Green+Zone&sn=001&sc=1000 (accessed 6 February 2008).
2. Ibid.

Chapter 21

1. A Yahoo! Contributer, comment on "What do you expect?," Yahoo! Travel, comment posted 14 July 2005, http://travel.yahoo.com/p-reviews-2514621-prod-hotel-action-read-ratings_and_reviews-i (accessed 16 March 2008).